HEART AFTER GOD

HEART AFTER GOD

Running With David

LUIS PALAU

MULTNOMAH PRESS
PORTLAND, OREGON 97266

© 1978 by Luis Palau

Published by Multnomah Press
Portland, Oregon 97266
Printed in the United States of America

The Library of Congress has provided the following CIP data for the trade paperback edition:
Palau, Luis, 1934–
   Heart after God: running with David / Luis Palau. — Portland, Or. : Multnomah Press, c1978.
   118 p. ; 22 cm.
   ISBN 0-930014-23-6

   1. David, King of Israel—Meditations.   I. Title.
BS580.D3P28   248'.4   78-57676
                                   MARC

Library of Congress   79

ISBN 0-930014-83-9

   85   86   87   88   89   90   91   –   9   8   7   6   5

Table of Contents

1. Where Kings Part Company 9

2. A Kingdom Canceled,
   a Kingdom Confirmed 19

3. The King's Shepherd 43

4. The Shepherd King 63

5. All the King's Horses . . .
   All the King's Men 85

6. "I Have Called You Friends" 101

7. David Had a Dream 123

8. A Sharp and Ready Arrow 143

Preface

While still a teen-ager, David was taking long strides toward greatness. His trail, though haunted by loneliness, tragedy, and broken dreams, climbed heights few have scaled since. David ran toward his God. Even today, his life gives birth to dreams. Young men and women who take time to unearth his footprints feel a tug at the feet to follow.

But the teen-age giant killer had giants to face as an adult, too. We read of David the great king, David the leader of nations, but we also read of a man with passions like our own who struggled and failed yet gathered up the broken pieces to give back to God. A man after God; a heart after God's heart.

David's dependence on spiritual resources coupled with his incessant forward action conquered a nation for God's purposes. Now, centuries later, the son of Jesse goes right on conquering lives and hearts for the Lord he loved and served.

David's life speaks with power to this generation. Facing almost impossible moral pressures and relentless assaults on the family, this generation needs to hear that a pattern of victory is possible. Utilizing principles practiced by David can provide us with God-appointed weapons.

In his triumph or in his failure, the son of Jesse teaches us. The message from David's life for this age is that we too can be men and women "after God's own heart."

A young man who has demonstrated his heart for God is Larry Libby. He has worked long and hard over this manuscript, not only as a technical professional but also with deep devotion of heart to our Lord Jesus Christ. My thanks also to Jeanne Doering who assisted Larry in this project of many months. I thank God that we are "workers together" with Christ (2 Corinthians 6:1).

And now, reader, may God be pleased to demonstrate through the life of this young king of Israel what He can do today through you. May He so mold your life that you will have a heart that beats in rhythm with His own.

Luis Palau
June, 1978

1

Where Kings
Part Company

The choices we make determine the shape and color of our lives.

Sometimes it's obvious. We stand at a well-marked crossroad and consciously, willfully, decide whether to take a right, a left, or plow straight ahead. Those are the kinds of choices we like. All the lights in a certain direction turn green at once, sunlight streams through the clouds in glorious confirmation, and a half-dozen smiling elders lay hands on our shoulders and give us Godspeed.

It doesn't work that way very often. Many of life's most crucial decisions occur in lonely, open fields where you can't even find rabbit tracks. Others are made in congested thoroughfares where it's so crowded your feet don't even touch the pavement as you move with the throng at the pedestrian crossing. Some decisions are far enough down the road that you have plenty of time to think about them before the road forks. Other decisions open suddenly at your feet, demanding instant action.

At such moments as these, when crisis flashes from a clear sky, *what* you know isn't as important as *who* you know. The important question to ask is not so much, "Am I walking in the right direction?", but rather, "Am I walking with the Director?" If you've been walking daily with the living God, drawing your life from Him, the crisis step is simply the next step.

"Here I am, Lord—instant decision time. You know that I want Your best in this so lead on! I'll be right behind."

If, on the other hand, you're walking in dependence on yourself—your own judgment —the crisis step can be terrifying. One wrong turn can alter a lifetime.

Two men, Saul and David, approached the same intersection together and parted company. One man ascended the stairs to unparalleled honor while the other fell broken and disgraced into the basement of obscurity.

The two of them had the same privileges, the same opportunities, the same background, and the same brilliant blessings of God. Yet only one of them found favor in the annals of Israel. Today the Star of *David* flutters proudly over the King *David* Hotel in Jerusalem. Think of it! After thirty centuries the name of David is esteemed all over the world, while Saul, Israel's first king, is somewhere back in the dim shadows.

Choices! All through life we approach critical, irreversible decisions. Only a few, momentary choices spelled the difference between the destiny of a Saul and the destiny of a David. It wasn't their environment. It wasn't their parents or their education, which separated their paths. It was the choices they made in the instant of crisis. And when you get down to the bottom line, that's making the difference in your life, too.

Both Saul and David felt the anointing oil of Samuel the prophet splash through their curls and trickle onto their broad shoulders while they were still young men.

Regarding Saul, Scripture says:

> *Now the day before Saul came, the LORD had revealed to Samuel: "Tomorrow about this time I will send to you a man from the land of Benjamin, and you shall anoint him to be prince over my people Israel. He shall save my people from the hand of the Philistines; for I have seen the affliction of my people, because their cry has come to me." When Samuel saw Saul, the LORD told him, "Here is the man of whom I spoke to you! He it is who shall rule over my people"* (1 Samuel 9:15-17).

Saul never sought the position of king. In that respect, he was like King George VI of England, and the American presidents Lyndon Johnson and Gerald Ford. Johnson acquired the office because of assassination. Ford, through resignation. George VI, through abdication. Saul was anointed, which means he was appointed! God chose Saul and said, "Saul shall be king in Israel."

David was God-appointed, too. The same prophet who poured the oil on Saul was sent out with another bottle to a Bethlehem address. At the right moment, God said to Samuel:

11

> *How long will you grieve over Saul, seeing I*
> *have rejected him from being king over Israel?*
> *Fill your horn with oil, and go; I will send you*
> *to Jesse the Bethlehemite, for I have provided for*
> *myself a king among his sons (1 Samuel 16:1).*

So the prophet visited Jesse and asked to see his sons. Seven of them filed past, one by one, as Samuel fingered his flowing gray beard. I can see old Samuel piercing the Bethlehemite with a steely stare from under his great, bushy eyebrows.

"Are you sure this is *all* of them?" the prophet rumbled.

"Well . . . *all* of them? Um . . . well . . . almost all of them . . . I mean . . . that is to say . . . not exactly all of them . . . there is one more out in the pasture—a mere child you understand—looking after a few sheep you understand. But you wouldn't . . . that is, he couldn't . . . er . . . a . . . we shouldn't. . . ."

"Bring him in!"

> *And he sent, and brought him in. Now he was*
> *ruddy, and had beautiful eyes, and was hand-*
> *some. And the LORD said, "Arise, anoint him;*
> *for this is he" (1 Samuel 16:12).*

"BORN AGAIN"

Not only were both Saul and David anointed, both of them also had a new-birth experience. Many people ask me, "Do you really think that Saul was 'born again'?" I answer *yes.* Even though his life ended in a tragic tangle of knots, the Scripture indicates that Saul had a second-birth experience.

Back a few chapters in 1 Samuel 10, Saul had an encounter with some prophets right after he was anointed. Samuel had said this would happen to verify that God had chosen the young Benjamite. Sketching verses 5-10:

> *"Afterward you will come to the hill of God . . . and be changed into another man" . . . God changed his heart . . . the Spirit of God came upon him . . . (NASB).*

Doesn't that mean Saul was born again? If God gives you a new heart and the Holy Spirit comes upon you, what more do you want? If that isn't being reborn, then I don't know what is.

We know David was reborn because the Lord says of him, "I have found in David the son of Jesse a man after my heart, who will do all my will" (Acts 13:22). Anybody who is in tune with God's own heart must have been born again.

ALL OF THIS AND GOOD LOOKS, TOO

Thirdly, both men enjoyed great physical advantages. In 1 Samuel 9:2, we read about Saul whom the Scripture portrays as:

> *. . . a handsome young man. There was not a man among the people of Israel more handsome than he; from his shoulders upward he was taller than any of the people.*

The son of Kish was a head-turner. Hollywood material. Towering head and shoulders above the crowd, he would have had pro basketball scouts lined up outside his door if he were around today. He had all the qualities, humanly speaking, that most of us look for in a leader.

"Now *there's* a leader," people will say. "Look how tall he is. And how about that mustache!" It doesn't always follow, but many people feel this way and the people of Israel were no exception.

A few years later we see David. Slightly younger than Saul at the time of his anointing, David's portrait is sketched in Scripture like this:

> *Now he was ruddy, and had beautiful eyes, and was handsome (1 Samuel 16:12).*

"Ruddy" really means sun-tanned. He had a healthy look to him. But there was something special about the suntan David wore. In fact, there was something special for everybody in David's looks. He was bronzed and brown so his mama thought he was good-looking, had beautiful eyes so the girls thought he was good-looking, and was handsome so even the men had to admit he was good-looking.

And, like Saul, this well-favored specimen was also filled with God's Holy Spirit from his youth.

HIDING IN THE BAGGAGE

Despite all their privileges, each of these men began their stellar careers with a truly humble attitude. Even as teenagers they weren't arrogant, pushy, or stomping all over other people.

Saul was so humble he almost missed his own coronation day. The people had gathered from all over Israel to see the big Benjamite crowned king.

The bands were playing and the flags were flying. But there was one person missing . . . Saul! Nobody could find him. Finally, someone spotted his large frame only half-hidden behind a trunk and a suit-bag in the back corner of a baggage room. Instead of strutting around signing autographs and kissing babies as any sensible politician would have done in a crowd like that, the intended king was trying to stay out of sight. Why was he hiding? Because he had a humble attitude. Even though he was hand-some, spiritually reborn, and divinely appointed to the throne, Saul felt unworthy and undeserving. He kept hoping it would all blow over so he could ride back to his dad's ranch in Benjamite country.

And when a bunch of "worthless fellows" mocked him and ridiculed his inauguration, Saul refused to retaliate.

"You think *he's* going to deliver us?" they jeered. "Ah, we're not going to give him anything but a hard time." Saul wasn't blind or thickheaded. He saw it and heard it. And he let it go. The Bible says he absolutely ignored them and kept silent.

We find the same attitude in David. Saul's effort to persuade the son of Jesse to marry one of his daughters is told in 1 Samuel 18. You'd have thought David would leap at the chance. To marry the king's daughter would mean privilege, position, and special opportunities by the score.

But look at the passage:

> And Saul commanded his servants, "Speak to David in private and say, 'Behold, the king has delight in you, and all his servants love you;

now then become the king's son-in-law.' " And
Saul's servants spoke those words in the ears of
David. And David said, "Does it seem to you a
little thing to become the king's son-in-law, see-
ing that I am a poor man and of no repute?"
(1 Samuel 18:22-23).

Even though he had known since his anointing
when he was a teen-ager that he would someday be
king, his heart remained humble.

They were all saying, "Come on, David. We all
love you. The king wants you in the family. And
have you seen his daughter? You're foolish if you
pass this up. You've got everything to gain and
nothing to lose. Now how about it?"

"It's no light thing to marry the king's daughter,"
David replied. "Me? Marry into the royal family?
You've got to be joking. Who am I? I'm just a shep-
herd and a poor shepherd at that."

David knew he was going to be king. And he was
popular—the talk of all Israel. He'd beaten Goliath
with a single stone and ballads on his bravery were
topping the charts from Dan to Beersheba. Yet because of his humility, David turned down Saul's ini-
tial offer to become a son-in-law.

WHAT'S THE DIFFERENCE?

The hand of God rested on both of these men in a
clear and unusual way. Both young kings were val-
iant generals and succeeded in beating and batter-
ing the enemies of Israel, in battle after battle. Both
were crowned near the same age. Both were hus-

bands. Both were fathers.

What tremendous young men they were! Privileged and blessed of God in every way. So you say to yourself, "What's the difference? Why do we remember David as a great man and Saul as a defeated man? Why did David's life climb up and up and Saul's plunge down and down? The name of David echoes through Scripture with splendor and power through . . . the Prophets . . . the Gospels . . . the Epistles . . . the Apocalypse. . . . But Saul? It's like someone padlocked the file. What happened?"

All of us know people who had everything going for them, people who started out strong. Loaded with talent, enthusiasm, and personality, their lives seemed to radiate potential for Christ. Everything was in their favor. Things were going great. Then suddenly—they drop out of sight. Talk floats back of a marriage breakup. Something happened that nobody wants to talk about because it's so embarrassing. And you wonder, what happened? What happened to Joe? Where's Mary these days? What happened?

Today is no different from the days of Saul and David. People are confronted by choices. Lives hinge on decisions forged in the heat of crisis. Some lives break loose from the moorings of mediocrity and sail new seas for the honor of Christ. Other lives bog down on sandbars and never make it out of the harbor.

With a couple of tragic exceptions, David made the right decisions at the right time. When a crisis rolled in like a sudden typhoon he was ready. He didn't need to panic and start thumbing madly through the phone book for God's number. He had it memorized a long time before. Out in the hills of Judah, alone with his sheep through the long nights, he dialed it frequently—and never found a busy signal. You can find many of their intimate conversations recorded in a book called *Psalms*.

Saul, slipping into the snare of self-reliance, carelessly left the phone off the hook. God couldn't get through to him. By the time the emergency was on top of the foolish king, it was too late.

How is it with your answering service? Disconnected? Maybe you've put God on "hold" and left Him there for years. Better clear the lines. There might be an emergency call waiting.

2

A Kingdom Canceled, a Kingdom Confirmed

It comes to our door in a variety of costumes, introducing itself by a number of different names: business failure, runaway child, serious illness, death. . . . When crisis comes—and it always comes—how do you meet it?

Most of us live like normal, regular, Smith-and-Jones kinds of people until crisis hurtles in and shatters our routine. People can learn a great deal about you by watching how you react in a moment of crisis. All the outward window dressing is jerked aside, revealing the reality of your walk with God. What are people learning about the sufficiency of Jesus Christ from observing your responses under sudden pressure?

When things are going smoothly, most of us can swing it. We can quote verses, sing hymns, show up at church, and stay more or less on tune. But when an emergency washes across our tranquil landscape—what then?

Ray Stedman likes to say, "Woe to the man who has to learn principles at a time of crisis." He should be learning those truths *before* the walls collapse. Otherwise, he'll be confused, overwhelmed, and constantly bullied around by his circumstances. His first reaction may be a long and bitter complaint directed against God.

"Oh, Lord . . . how could you allow this to happen? How does a God of love permit this? I've been faithful to the church. I've given my money to the carpet fund. If God can't help me now—I'm quitting! If this is the way God pays me. . . ."

Suddenly Mr. Pillar-of-the-Church begins to sound just like his pagan neighbor. It happens all too often. Usually in the heat of crisis. At that point, at that decisive instant, a choice must be made. How we choose to respond at that crossroads could either pump fresh faith into our spiritual veins or set us back ten years in our witness and our walk with God.

Do you find yourself blaming God when the furnace of affliction begins to heat up? Saul did. When the pressure was on, we find Saul immediately acting as if he'd never known the Lord.

What a difference, though, with David. When he was persecuted, rather than blaming the Lord, David would say, "Well, the Lord knows I deserve to be persecuted." When he had to hide, he would say, "The Lord knows why I have to hide." He related every event in his life to the hand of the Lord.

The fall of Saul cannot be traced to one awful, dramatic, disastrous, instantaneous failure. Few people ever fail that way. With Saul, it was a series of wrong turns which brought his life and his kingdom to ruin. Wrong choice after wrong choice. Wrong response after wrong response. Missing the right turn at one crucial intersection, Saul would panic and take one wrong turn after another. Instead of going back to the place where he first lost his direction, he kept getting in deeper.

Let's try to trace his route. We know his eventual destination: failure, folly, suicide. But how did he end up at a place like that? How did a man with such a brilliant future end up in such a dark and hopeless back alley?

WRONG TURN NO. 1: IMPATIENCE

One of Saul's most damaging dead-end routes bore a road sign reading: "Impatience." Look at 1 Samuel 13. Saul and his men were preparing for war against the Philistine army, which had the Israelite camp surrounded. Tension was high, and Saul was eager to attack. Then, just when everything seemed ripe to launch an offensive, Samuel the prophet left for seven days. It was time for the sacrifice to be offered before battle, but Samuel was out of town.

Before he departed, the old prophet left the king with a firm directive. "Wait until I return," Samuel told him. "When I get back in seven days, we'll offer a sacrifice to the Lord and after that we'll go to war. Then the Lord will give us the victory."

Day one passed. Everyone was getting nervous. Captains of the troops kept riding in to report that the soldiers' morale was ebbing and couldn't something be done soon? Day two. Day three. Day four. The enemy was only on the other side of the hill and the anticipation had everyone itchy. You could cut the tension in camp with a knife. Even the mules were restless. Still no Samuel. Day six. Some of the people began to walk out on Saul, heading back home. In the meantime, the king was becoming feverishly impatient.

"Where is that old man? What kind of time is this to take a holiday?"

Day seven.

Piling wood on the altar, Saul decided to "get things ready" for Samuel. Daylight revealed that still more soldiers had deserted the Israelite cause. The sun climbed higher in the sky and still the prophet tarried.

Finally Saul could stand it no longer. Maybe something had happened to the old man. He *had* to get the troops out and fighting. Wasn't that a king's responsibility? So even though Samuel was the only one supposed to offer sacrifices, Saul said:

> *"Bring the burnt offering here to me, and the peace offerings." And he offered the burnt offering (1 Samuel 13:9).*

Just as he was finishing, Samuel came striding into camp. Saul hurried to meet him.

"What have you done?" Samuel asked.

Listen how Saul tried to justify his actions.

> *"When I saw that the people were scattering from me, and that you did not come within the days appointed, and that the Philistines had mustered at Michmash, I said, 'Now the Philistines will come down upon me at Gilgal, and I have not entreated the favor of the LORD'; so I forced myself, and offered the burnt offering" (1 Samuel 13:11-12).*

Samuel wasn't one to waste time on niceties. He called the king of Israel a fool.

> *"You have done foolishly; you have not kept the commandment of the LORD your God, which he commanded you; for now the LORD would have established your kingdom over Israel for ever. But now your kingdom shall not continue; the LORD has sought out a man after his own heart; and the LORD has appointed him to be prince over his people, because you have not kept what the LORD commanded you" (1 Samuel 13:13-14).*

Having delivered Saul this devastating blow, the old prophet wheeled around and walked out of camp, leaving the king standing open-mouthed before the smoldering altar.

You and I might say that what Saul did wasn't so bad. It was just a simple matter of rushing ahead of the Lord *a little*, right? The enemy armies were surrounding him. The seventh day had come and the prophet hadn't shown. So what do you do? Saul simply took matters into his own hands and kindled the sacrifice on his own.

Impatience. How many of us have ruined rare and unusual opportunities to serve Christ because of impatience? It doesn't seem like such a big thing and yet—do you know what impatience represents? *It is a sign of distrust in the sovereign control of God.* We demonstrate by our hasty actions that we really don't believe our God is in loving control of every event which enters our lives. Impatience, then, is another word for *unbelief*.

We jump the gun and insist on beating the Lord to the draw. Somehow we become convinced that our God has lost control of the circumstances in our lives. Or that He really doesn't care.

"My soul," we say, "the whole thing's falling apart! I'm going to have to intervene in this myself. If the Lord can't handle it, well, I surely can. I've been to college. I've had experience. Let me at it."

Through the years, my wife and I have seen a number of couples and families become ensnared in this trap called impatience. I think of one young couple in particular. The Lord seemed to be opening doors for them, using their lives in a clear and visible way. Then they got impatient. It wasn't happening fast enough for them. They wanted to move on. Their pastor saw some serious problems with their proposed move and advised them, "Don't go." We were their friends and one night we were at their home for dinner. As they asked for counsel, we told them, "Don't go." Many other people in the church also said, "Don't go. Don't go."

But no. "God was leading." They just wouldn't wait. Against all advice, they packed up and moved.

What happened? It wasn't long before things began to fall apart. The man lost his job. The woman became confused and unhappy. They began to fight and lost all chance of ministry. Why? They were simply too impatient to wait for the Lord's time. They had received counsel to wait from those who loved them. All the circumstances said, "Hang in there. Wait for the Lord's best time." But they had to jump right in.

Refusing to wait for God's green light, King Saul leaped straight into disaster. Impatience is no joke. Unbelief is a grief to the heart of God. Apart from the empowering presence of the indwelling Christ, this sin of impatience could be *my* downfall. Or yours. For Saul, it was the first wrong turn which led directly to another one.

WRONG TURN NO. 2: PARTIAL OBEDIENCE

Wheeling down the road of impatience, it was an easy matter for Saul to merge onto the broad highway of disobedience.

Back on the battlefield again, the king was preparing to make a strike against Israel's long-time adversary, the Amalekites. God had said, "The Amalekites are my enemies. I want them totally destroyed —every living thing. They refused to help the children of Israel as they came out of Egypt. And now, these many years later, they are totally corrupt. Let nothing live—wipe out everything." The instructions were clear.

So Saul and his armies marched on the Amalekites and destroyed them . . . almost. They demolished everything . . . except . . . they did not kill the king, they saved the best of the livestock, and they kept a few good things like gold and treasures. The rest—the junk of the land—they dutifully burned and destroyed. So the smoke billowed from the villages of the Amalekites, but the Israelites marched out with a few little goodies because they figured these were too nice and too good. And besides, you wouldn't want to kill a king.

25

Was God pleased with this "interpretation" of His command? Look at the record:

> The word of the LORD came to Samuel: "I repent that I have made Saul king; for he has turned back from following me, and has not performed my commandments."
>
> And Samuel was angry; and he cried to the LORD all night. And Samuel rose early to meet Saul in the morning; and it was told Samuel, "Saul came to Carmel, and behold, he set up a monument for himself and turned, and passed on, and went down to Gilgal."
>
> And Samuel came to Saul, and Saul said to him, "Blessed be you to the LORD; I have performed the commandment of the LORD."
>
> And Samuel said, "What then is this bleating of the sheep in my ears, and the lowing of the oxen which I hear?" (1 Samuel 15:10-14).

You'll notice that Saul's actions weren't *total disobedience*. It wasn't as if he had said, "Look, Samuel. I just don't have the heart to kill these Amalekites. No sir. That's a nasty little job—too much bloodshed. I will not do it." No, he didn't say that.

He did what he was told—with just a few exceptions. It wasn't out-and-out insubordination. It was partial obedience. He didn't carry out the full instructions.

In the same way, it usually isn't gross sin or blatant immorality which sinks many Christians. It is "almost obedience." Notice that God did not take

Saul's partial obedience lightly. "What you have done is rebellion!" He said through Samuel.

Rebellion? Isn't that a little strong? That's what Saul thought.

"*Who* rebelled? Not me, Samuel. I went on the mission. I killed the Amalekites. The whole place is in flames. So we kept a few sheep and cows and didn't kill the king. Is that such a big thing?"

But the Lord had said, "Do it all." It wasn't up to Saul to decide what he was going to do and what he wasn't going to do. The Lord hadn't asked for evaluation or interpretation. He asked for obedience.

> Samuel went on, "When you were little in your own sight, did you not become a prince of Israel's tribes, and has not the Lord anointed you to be king over Israel? The Lord sent you out under orders. He said: Go and destroy the evildoers, the Amalekites; fight them until you have exterminated them. Why then, did you not listen to the Lord's voice, but flung yourself on the loot and did evil in the Lord's sight?" (1 Samuel 15:17-19 MLB).

There must have been sorrow in the prophet's voice as he confronted the disobedient king. Samuel's sorrow and God's sorrow.

"Oh Saul, son of Kish, the Lord chose you, singled you out from among all the tribes of Israel. Though you were small and unimportant in your own sight the God of your fathers selected you for unprecedented blessing. He poured out honor and privilege and favor upon you even as I poured the anointing oil over your head. But more than that, He poured Himself into your life. He gave you His own Spirit as Companion, Guide, and never-failing Fountain of strength. How then could you turn your back on all that to satisfy your own selfish desires?"

Saul adapted God's Word to suit his own plans. He rearranged it to fit his own life style, doing such a clever job that he almost fooled himself.

"Wait a minute!" he cried. "I *did* obey the Lord. I wiped out those Amalekites. See—here is their king and here are their best animals which we want to sacrifice to the Lord."

> *And Samuel said, "Has the LORD as great delight in burnt offerings and sacrifices, as in obeying the voice of the LORD? Behold, to obey is better than sacrifice, and to hearken than the fat of rams.*
>
> *"For rebellion is as the sin of divination, and stubbornness is as iniquity and idolatry. Because you have rejected the word of the LORD, he has also rejected you from being king"* (1 Samuel 15:22-23).

It's the same with us. God isn't interested in our fanfare and flashy spiritual speeches. What He wants is our simple obedience. All the way—from the heart.

As our evangelistic team travels worldwide, we've seen it in the lives of many, many believers. Partial obedience. Maybe you break with some sinful things that you don't like, anyway. But you hang onto a few selected goodies. You say, "Well, let's not be extremists. Surely a little is all right." Of course, you wouldn't do too much. Just a little playing around. "No, I wouldn't be caught in a strip joint, but reading a little light pornography isn't going to hurt anybody. It's just a piece of paper. And watching this questionable TV program isn't that bad. You have to know how the world thinks, don't you? It's not like you're going all out. . . ."

So you give an inch here, a foot there, and before you know it you're out of the race. You've lost the power, you've lost the anointing.

Although Saul continued to be king in the technical sense, in reality his kingdom was canceled. From then on nobody paid much attention to him. People knew he was finished. Even his own son said, "My dad doesn't have it anymore." Having drifted so far from God's chosen course, Saul burned out and dead-ended on the back roads . . . the wrong roads.

"Rebellion," says the Scripture, "is as the sin of divination, and stubbornness is as iniquity and idolatry." In other words, in God's sight, rebellion is like going into the occult. We shake our heads when we read about someone dabbling in the occult, don't we? And we say, "Oh, the occult, uh—oh. . . ." Of course, we ought to be afraid of the occult. But God says when we rebel—that is, when knowingly we partially obey—that is the same as consorting with demons.

And then He says, "Stubbornness is as iniquity and idolatry." We may be horrified to see someone praying to a statue of a saint. Or shocked to see some savage bowing to the sun and the moon. But the Bible says that stubbornness before God is the same as falling on your face before Buddha. Has the Lord been speaking to you about a particular area of your life? Be careful if you are considering the route of stubborn resistance.

WRONG TURN NO. 3:
OATHS, THREATS, AND CURSES

By the time we arrive in 1 Samuel 14, all the phone lines between Saul and his God have been severed. The Holy Spirit has removed His hand of blessing from the unhappy king. The wrong turns come easier now—with increasing frequency.

The scene opens in the midst of another battle with the Philistines. Relying on his own strength and wisdom—out of touch with God —Saul made a very foolish oath:

> *And the men of Israel were distressed that day; for Saul laid an oath on the people, saying, "Cursed be the man who eats food until it is evening and I am avenged on my enemies." So none of the people tasted food (1 Samuel 14:24).*

Saul's son, Jonathan, hadn't heard about the curse. As the battle stretched on through the day, a number of the Israelites passed through a forest where honeycomb was in abundance. Exhausted and famished, Jonathan speared a piece with the end of his staff and chewed on it as the troops maneuvered through the trees. The effect of the honey was instantaneous. Verse 27 says he "put his hand to his mouth; and his eyes became bright."

It must have been obvious. Among the bone-weary, half-starved soldiers of Israel, Jonathan's bright eyes shone like beacons.

> *Then one of the people said, "Your father strictly charged the people with an oath, saying, 'Cursed be the man who eats food this day.'"*
>
> *And the people were faint. Then Jonathan said, "My father has troubled the land; see how my eyes have become bright, because I tasted a little of this honey. How much better if the people had eaten freely today of the spoil of their enemies which they found; for now the slaughter among the Philistines has not been great" (1 Samuel 14:28-30).*

That very evening Saul was ready to execute his own son for violating his foolish, arbitrary oath against eating. At that point, however, the citizen soldiers of Israel mounted an overwhelming protest against the actions of their king and rescued Jonathan from the murderous intentions of his father.

"You're not going to touch a hair of this young man's head!" they told Saul. And that was that. But if the people hadn't saved the young prince, King Saul would have run him through with a sword.

What a weird thing to do. While Jonathan was fighting his heart out, claiming the strength of God to scatter the enemy, Saul was dreaming up oaths and curses that God never demanded. Saul thought he was acting spiritual, but he was only acting. He was completely out of touch with God, and all his "holy" oaths and regulations were a sham and a show.

I know of parents who think they are being ultra-spiritual with their regulations when actually they are miles away from God and His Word. One day at a place in California where I was speaking, a beautiful girl about nineteen years old came for counsel. She was from a Christian family. But her face was troubled.

"Mr. Palau, there is deep tension in our home. In a few days my older sister, who is only twenty, is going to pack up and leave. She really can't afford to but she's leaving anyway."

"Why?" I asked.

"Well," she said, "my dad puts restrictions on us that are ridiculous. We don't have big shouting matches, but my sister can't take him any more."

"Give me an example," I said.

"Well, ever since he went to a Christian seminar where he was taught that the father is over the daughter, he has come on so strong that we're hardly allowed to breathe without consulting him. I mean, we even have to ask his permission to go buy a hamburger, and we're nineteen and twenty.

"My sister has a nice, Christian boyfriend from our church. But Dad said that whenever she wants to see him they always have to stay where he can see them both—at all times. He told them, 'I don't want you going for a walk behind my back.' My sister says, 'Dad, we're not going to be doing anything wrong. We just want to *talk*.' But Dad says, 'The Scripture says to obey your father. Now you stay where I can see you.' "

I couldn't believe it. That kind of oath—that sort of restriction—is unreasonable. Proverbs 26:2 says that a curse without a cause never comes to pass. You can take Scripture and twist it around to bolster your own ego—making it say things that God never intended. That's what this girl's father did and that's what Saul did. Saul had drifted so far from the mind and heart of God that he was making absurd, pointless rulings to massage his own ego. "I'm the king!" he said. "I have a right. Everybody should submit to my chain of command. Whoever touches any food today—he's finished. He is under a curse." So nobody ate. And Israel could have lost the war.

WRONG TURN NO. 4: "A MONUMENT TO MYSELF"

Notice that Saul built for himself a self-exalting monument. Look at 1 Samuel 15:12:

> And Samuel rose early to meet Saul in the morning; and it was told Samuel, "Saul came to Carmel, and behold, he set up a monument for himself and turned, and passed on, and went down to Gilgal."

What a contrast to David. Do you know what David lived for all his life? To build a monument. But it wasn't one for himself. Remember what it was? The temple. In all his life, David never made money for himself, never grabbed for riches, never appropriated anything. His one big dream in life was to build a temple for the Ark of the Lord. He would lie awake at night and think about it. It was his deepest-felt desire. But what was Saul's desire? To build a monument for himself.

What kind of monument are you building? What will your children see when you've made your exit from the scene? A monument to yourself? A self-serving life that catered to your own desires and your own ego? The landscape is dotted with those sorts of monuments. But you have to watch them close—they fade very fast. There are other monuments that can be erected in your life—monuments that will continue to bring honor to the name of God's Son throughout eternity. I ask you again: What kind of monument are you building?

WRONG TURN NO. 5: DISLOYALTY

As the wick on Saul's reign burned lower and lower, even his loyalty to loved ones began to flicker and fade. He was disloyal to his son Jonathan and to his friend, protector, and best soldier, David. We've already seen 1 Samuel 14:39, where Saul said:

> *"For as the LORD lives who saves Israel, though it be in Jonathan my son, he shall surely die."*

As if he was making some statement of grand dedication to God! Saul was a bitter, defeated man sputtering a silly, useless curse. On his own son! That demonstrates the degree to which Saul was disloyal to his own family. No compassion—no mercy. All he wanted was his own way, to some-how reestablish himself in the eyes of the people.

34

But everyone saw through that bit of self-serving hypocrisy!

Remember how many times David fought for Saul, demonstrating kindness and loyalty to the king? (Even though he knew Saul was on the way out.) Yet Saul was so envious of David that he tried to murder him. Friendship was expendable. Loyalty was expendable. Family ties were expendable. Anything to stay on top of the pile. Anything to defend the ego and look good in the eyes of other people. By the time a man has reached that length of rutted road, it becomes extremely difficult to turn back. The bridges are burned behind. It's almost too late. Almost. Fortunately, Jeremiah 32:27 is still in the Bible:

> "Behold, I am the LORD, the God of all flesh; is anything too hard for me?"

WRONG TURN NO. 6: JEALOUSY

One small seed of jealousy, once it takes root in the soil of the soul, can sprout overnight into a sprawling vine of poison ivy. Its choking tentacles reach into every corner of the inner man, spreading poison and bitter stench as they go. In the latter days of his kingdom, you could hardly recognize the original Saul. He was thoroughly cocooned in the vines of envy and revenge.

The beginnings of this cancerous weed in Saul's heart are traced in 1 Samuel 18:5-9. The Scripture states that whenever David went to fight, he was successful. When the young warrior returned from upending the Philistine champion, women from across Israel came out singing, dancing, and playing musical instruments. Their song?

> *Saul has slain his thousands,*
> *And David his ten thousands . . . (1 Samuel*
> *18:7).*

The tune was an immediate hit. Young girls sang it in the streets. Soldiers whistled it in formation. Housewives hummed it washing their clothes in the river. Every time Saul heard the song, it was like smoke in his eyes and sand in his teeth.

> *And Saul was very angry, and this saying dis-*
> *pleased him; he said, "They have ascribed to*
> *David ten thousands, and to me they have as-*
> *cribed thousands; and what more can he have*
> *but the kingdom?" And Saul eyed David from*
> *that day on (1 Samuel 18:8-9).*

Hatred and jealousy welled up inside the suspicious king. His mind worked constantly, thinking of ways to destroy the young man who was gaining such high regard among the people. Jealousy always leads to an attempt to destroy the other person. We have to be watchful for the first appearance of this damaging weed in our own gardens.

I'm an evangelist, and the Lord has blessed my work. We've seen thousands come to Christ. We've preached to millions. But I really have to watch my heart when I read in a magazine or newspaper about some other young evangelist who is being used in a mighty way by the Lord. Now what is it to me if some Asian evangelist has a big campaign?

Yet, before I realize what's going on, I find myself saying, "Ah, he didn't have that many people at his crusade. I'll bet they reported it 'evangelistically speaking.' " It's a tremendous temptation to demean this servant of the Lord whom I've never met, simply because he is successful.

I have no problem with Billy Graham, because he's obviously bigger. But when it's some young evangelist—some new "Third World" preacher — and someone fills my ears with all he's doing . . . then it becomes difficult.

"Did you hear about this guy in Africa?" someone will say. "They say he had a million people saved in the last ten years." When I hear something like that I have a tendency to wince, thinking, "Come on now. It can't be a million people." I really have to watch it so this monster jealousy doesn't start working on me. I have to take it to the Lord Jesus and say, "Oh God, forgive me. After all these years of knowing better, I still have this thing creep up on me."

You may not be an evangelist and so you say, "That's not *my* problem." But perhaps jealousy sneaks into your life by a different door. Maybe some girl you know is sharper than you and you know it and there's no way you can get around it. She's slim—eats all she wants and never gets fat — and you put on weight eating lettuce and drinking weak tea.

So you find yourself thinking, "I *know* she has a problem. Maybe she doesn't take care of her children." Then you find out that this sharp, slim lady keeps a good house, has happy, well-behaved kids, and also teaches at a junior college twice a week.

Your mind keeps working and working. You say to yourself, "It just can't be. She must have a major failing somewhere. Maybe she and her husband don't get along."

Jealousy begins to filter through your pores as you try harder and harder to find fault with the other person and, in effect, murder her. Not with a gun or a knife. You don't have what it takes. But with words—the venomous fruit of the envy vine. At least in your mind you can slay that other individual.

What a destructive force, this jealousy. Like the son of Kish, many Christians have found their life potential for Jesus Christ blighted or blotted out because they gave the treacherous voice of jealousy a hearing in their souls. Don't let it speak! Stop it before it utters one vile word. Perhaps in the silence that follows you'll be able to discern the still, small voice of the One who loves you—just as you are.

THE BEAUTY OF BROKENNESS

Is it really so surprising that Saul was tempted with impatience, disobedience, making oaths, pride, disloyalty, and jealousy? I don't think so. I have the same temptations. Maybe you have a few. David experienced them, too. But David kept going up while Saul kept going down. Why? Do you know the real difference between Saul and David? It's simple. Never in Saul's life do you find him humbling himself and confessing that he had sinned against the Lord—and really meaning it.

One time there was a confession. Samuel said to

Saul, "I'm going to leave you." Saul grabbed the prophet's coat and said, "I have sinned against the Lord. Please come and honor me before the people." But it was a fake confession. He only said it to pacify the prophet. What he really wanted was his honor back. He wasn't repenting. He wasn't broken before God. He wasn't confessing his sin. Saul couldn't stand to be humiliated in the eyes of the people. He would have confessed anything to Samuel to salvage his ego.

When the finger of guilt pointed at the deserving king, he usually found ways to dodge or tip it in another direction. He never broke down. Every time, he accused other people. He found excuses.

"Sure hated to take matters in my own hands and offer that sacrifice, but the people, Samuel, those disloyal soldiers of mine, were deserting! What's a king to do? Besides that—hate to remind you, Samuel—you kept delaying and delaying your promised return. A day or two I could see, but a *week*, Samuel? What choice did I have? Unhappy me—I had to force myself to perform your duties. . . . What's that, Samuel? You hear bleating sheep and lowing oxen? It must be these special, pick-of-the-flock animals which I brought along for sacrifices. I saw all that fine livestock and I thought to myself, 'Saul, that is fine livestock. It would be a shame to waste it when we could sacrifice it to the Lord.' So we herded them all the way here—ready for the altar. Yes sir, we went to a lot of trouble but—no sacrifice is too great. Right, Samuel? Samuel? . . . "

Shifting the blame is as old as Adam, who blamed Eve, or Eve, who in turn blamed the serpent. Pause for a moment to consider your own life. Could it be you've sensed a real spiritual decline in the last few years? Perhaps your family has been going through a time of stormy tension and instead of saying, "I am to blame," you keep dodging around and pointing at someone else. "It's my wife," you say, "if only she were different." Or, "It's that mother-in-law of mine, these rebellious kids, that uncaring pastor, that cold, lifeless church . . ." and on and on. Anybody but yourself. That was Saul's stumbling block. You rarely find him confessing, "I have sinned against the Lord." You never find him broken.

David, God's man, committed some sins that were actually more terrible than anything Saul had done. But whenever a prophet or someone else confronted him and said, "David, you've done it, man," David would crumble. Falling on his face he would cry, "I've sinned against my God! Oh Lord, have mercy on this sinner." And he would mean it to the depth of his soul. He would confess it all and strive to make it right with God. Then the Lord would say, "All right. You've repented. You're broken. You've confessed. You're forgiven. David, keep going."

"David is a man after my own heart," God would say. But not Saul. The ultimate, irreparable decision for Saul was that there was no brokenness, no repentance, and therefore no forgiveness. The Lord gave him chance after chance to change, to turn around. Again and again He sent Samuel. But proud Saul could not admit defeat, or failure, or sin. "I'll tough it out," he thought. "I'll weather the storm and come out of this somehow." He didn't make it.

Which are you—a Saul or a David? Are you a Saul who was king and top man on the outside—but dead in your heart, dead in your soul? Or are you a David, willing to accept a slip in public image, willing to be marred in men's eyes if only to be right with God?

If you want to be a David, get alone with your God. Tell Him, "I want to begin life right here, again. Not like Saul, blaming everyone else, pretending, living on a past anointing. But like the son of Jesse . . . willing to be broken . . . cleansed by the blood of Christ . . . living in the light, with my heart set on doing the will of God."

The way to God's heart is the way of brokenness. David walked it, Saul wouldn't. Will you?

3

The King's Shepherd

The "apple" is the very center of the eye. In Old Testament days, when they talked about hurting someone, they spoke of injuring "the apple of his eye." That was bad. Back then there were no bifocals, contact lenses, or ophthalmologists. If you hurt your eye, it was finished —and so were you. That's why people jealously protected their eyes.

The name *David* means "the apple of God's eye." David was the apple of God's eye, beloved of God because he was "a man after God's own heart." And because of this his life was marked by greatness. Ever wonder why God included David's biography in the Bible? It wasn't because it was just an interesting story. Nor was God saying, "Okay, here's the story of My special person. I want you to read it and feel guilty because you'll never measure up—you'll never make it." No! As someone has said, "Most books are written for our *information*, the Bible was written for our *transformation*." Romans 15:4 says:

> For whatever was written in former days was written for our instruction, that by steadfast-

*ness and by the encouragement of the scriptures
we might have hope.*

The story of David was recorded to give us encouragement and hope! God loves to walk with men. He longs to speak to the responsive heart. The way to God's heart is wide open through Jesus Christ. The chronicle of David is simply an account of how one sinful, stumbling human being responded to the grace and love of his Creator. It can be your story, too. I pray that it will be mine. But what was it that so endeared this man David to his God? What qualities of David's life made him live up to his name as "the apple of God's eye"?

A Thirst for God

In 1 Samuel 13, God told the grieving prophet that He would seek out a man after His own heart to take Saul's place on the throne. God is continually looking for people who say, "Oh Lord, I want my heart to be a heart after Your own."

It has nothing to do with whether you're fat or thin, black or white, woman or man, young or old. God is looking at you and saying, "Can I use this person? Can I really use this person for My glory? Can I really work through him? Can I give him more opportunities to express the Gospel, win people to My Son, and build up My Body? Is this person's heart after My own heart? If it is, then I'll keep opening doors for him—I'll use him more and more every day."

God spread an impressive array of opportunities

before this young man, David. He was probably eighteen years old when he was anointed to be the founder of the royal line from which Jesus Christ came. Think of it! Out in the pastures among the grazing sheep, God was preparing this teen-ager to be the founder of Messiah's line. What an unspeakable privilege.

A lot of adults look at teen-agers today and say, "Oh, those crazy kids." Maybe they are crazy, but there is a lot of beautiful stuff inside those young people—beautiful potential. Certainly there is an ugly side, too—as there is in all of us—and that has to be taken care of by the Lord. But I think David must have gotten the same rub-off when he was a teen-ager. He was the youngest of eight brothers, and, like normal older brothers, they put him down. When the prophet Samuel came to their ranch house in Bethlehem, they didn't even invite David to the party.

"David? The runt? He's just a kid. He's out with the sheep. Don't bother about him."

But from God's perspective, the "kid" David was one of the most important persons in His vast plan of the ages. God looked at David's heart. To his brothers, David was just an irresponsible kid, a wild teen-ager who beat up lions and scared bears. But God was looking beneath the exterior—and saw a spirit that hungered after Him.

Later on, David became *the* national hero. He came back from leveling Goliath and all the people scrambled to get on the "David bandwagon." If it happened today, David tee-shirts, sweat tops, and bicycle decals would be selling faster than department stores could keep them in stock. All the women and girls of Israel sang his praises. But did this mean much to God? Remember 1 Samuel 16:7? "The LORD sees not as man sees; man looks on the outward appearance, but the LORD looks on the heart." If God sees a heart that is yearning for His presence, there is no blessing that He will withhold.

David was desperate for God. You see it in his life. You hear it in his music:

> As the deer pants for the water brooks,
> So my soul pants for Thee, O God.
> My soul thirsts for God, for the living God;
> When shall I come and appear before God?
>   (Psalm 42:1-2 NASB).

> O God, Thou art my God; I shall seek Thee
>   earnestly;
> My soul thirsts for Thee, my flesh yearns for
>   Thee,
> In a dry and weary land where there is no water
>   (Psalm 63:1 NASB).

David had the incurable habit of bringing every situation in life to his God. Whether it was a battle, a family decision, a nameless fear, a crushing sorrow, or a cherished dream—whatever it was, the first thing David said was, "I'm going to talk to the Lord about it." Not that he was some grim-faced grit-your-teeth, pious disciplinarian: "Ah, there's the alarm clock. Have to do my devotions. Have to drag myself out of bed and go through the ritual." None of that at all! With David, it was a natural thing. As soon as the opportunity came up, he spoke with the

Lord. In other words, he related everything in his life to the Person of God. He didn't *do* his devotions; he *lived* them.

Take a minute to think through your day, as far as it has progressed. Think about your activities, your words, your purchases, your decisions. How often did you consult your God? How many times today have you paused in your frantic pace to seek the counsel of the One you call "Lord"? Whether you're a businessman, career woman, housewife, college student, or high schooler, you've got to get used to the concept. If we want God to use us in a powerful way, we must have a heart for Him—for His desires, His commands. Everything we do, no matter how trivial or mundane it seems, must relate to His presence and His Person. Then we will realize His blessing.

When it comes to a marriage partner, count on God's provision. Set your heart on God's selection and God's timing. Allow Him to bring along the right man or woman at the right time. Don't take it casually, decide on somebody, and say, "God, bless so-and-so. I love him. He's got the right kind of eyes. He's ruddy and all the rest of it." Then you pray, pray, pray. But it's a tacked-on prayer. You made your decision before coming to God, instead of the other way around. You're playing games with God. And you may find trouble later on. Deep trouble.

When it comes to money, take the matter to God. Moving from one city to another, take it to God. Changing jobs, really put it before God. Planning a vacation, consult the Lord. You may react, "I'll turn into a fanatic if I start putting God into everything. Only the lunatic fringe does that." But neglecting to include God in your plans is precisely the reason why so much trouble, agony, and suffering prevail on our planet—because people think they don't have to relate their everyday lives to their God. David would bitterly agree. The few times he neglected to seek God on a matter nearly devastated his life and his family. The chain reaction of pain and sorrow sparked by those few selfish moments gave David pangs for the rest of his life.

A PENETRATING DISCERNMENT

To find out what happened in David's life, we can read the books of Samuel. If we want to know what went on in his mind, we can turn to his own very personal songbook . . . the Psalms.

Psalm 37 reveals one of David's unusual inner qualities. In that psalm, David says, "Don't fret yourself because of evil people. Don't worry about the outward appearance. Don't worry about those who prosper and appear to be right even though they are pagans. Don't worry. Their end is coming. They may appear to be well off, but God hasn't settled His accounts yet."

David made that crucial distinction between outward appearance and the heart. Christians are often tempted to think, "Well, look at that man over there. Here I walk with God. I give my tithe to God. I train my children right. And I can hardly cut it at the end of the month. Yet my neighbor over there is a crook. He drinks and runs around. Look at him.

He's got money for everything. He can do anything he wants. What's going on?"

In many of the psalms, David says, "Listen, take time to go into the sanctuary and get yourself in the presence of God. Soon you'll find out that outward appearance is nothing. What counts is inward reality."

It's good to know that when you're a teen-ager. You know—you go to school and bump into Mr. Muscle or Miss Slick Chick, the hotshots who push themselves around. They're the girls with a new outfit every week. Or the guys with all the muscles who wear the sleeveless shirts to show them off. Maybe you're skinny and wear long sleeves, or else you're short and stubby. But they can do anything. If they go to the beach they get a suntan. You go and come back burned and blotchy or peeling like a banana. If they swim, they win the races. If they water ski, they can do it on one—you can't do it with three. Everything seems to go right for them while everything goes upside-down for you.

But the outward appearance doesn't mean much to God. He's looking at your heart. If in your youth God sees a heart that is after His own heart, it will be you who sees the blessing when the full story is told.

A Sensitive Spirit

It's not unusual for a man to possess power. Neither is it unusual for power to possess a man. Men and kings are not judged so much for the authority they wield, but rather for how that authority wields them. In the course of history, many men have found themselves in positions of leadership and command. Some are born to it. Others are elected to it. Still others seize it. Most simply claw their way to the top through long, weary years of sacrifice and toil. All of that is soon forgotten. What is remembered is how that man exercised the power once he held it.

God chose Saul to reign. Saul chose to reign without God. In Saul's hand, the authority of the king became hard, brittle, arbitrary, and cruel. Saul held the scepter but the scepter held him. He issued commands simply to command. Clinging to the power of his office, he forfeited the greatest power of all: the presence of God's Spirit. Knowing in his heart that his sovereignty was hollow, the frustrated king rattled his saber all the louder and sought to kill the man who possessed what he had foolishly let slip away.

David, hunted and hounded through years of his early manhood, also found himself in a position of power. In 1 Samuel 24, the Lord placed the life of his mortal enemy, Saul, within his grasp.

> When Saul returned from following the Philistines, he was told, "Behold, David is in the wilderness of Engedi." Then Saul took three thousand chosen men out of all Israel, and went to seek David and his men in front of the Wildgoats' Rocks. And he came to the sheepfolds by the way, where there was a cave; and Saul went in to relieve himself. Now David and his men were sitting in the innermost parts of

the cave (1 Samuel 24:1-3).

Perfect opportunity. What a choice moment for David to rise up and put an end to the man who had sworn to kill him. Saul was unarmed, unsuspecting, and helpless. David's men were going out of their heads for joy. Here was the moment they'd been waiting for. They could hardly keep from shouting. One of them took David aside and whispered tensely:

> *Here is the day of which the LORD said to you,*
> *"Behold, I will give your enemy into your hand,*
> *and you shall do to him as it shall seem good to*
> *you" (1 Samuel 24:4).*

Why did David delay? "Go get him," they said through clenched teeth. "Butcher him. Cut him down. He's in your hand!" The young shepherd crawled forward in the darkness and snipped off a piece of Saul's robe with his razor-sharp dagger. He could just as easily have slipped it between Saul's ribs. David's men must have been stunned with their leader's reaction as he crept back into the depths of the cavern.

> *And afterward David's heart smote him, be-*
> *cause he had cut off Saul's skirt (1 Samuel*
> *24:5).*

Just cutting a piece of the king's robe overwhelmed David's tender conscience. He had touched his knife to the king of Israel—he had reached out his hand against the Lord's anointed one. It was too much. David forced his men to lie

51

still and let Saul make his exit from the cave. The power had been in David's hand to take vengeance. But David chose to surrender that power to God.

He said, in effect, "If anyone is going to kill Saul it will have to be the Lord, not me. I will not use this moment of power to satisfy my own vengeance. I will not touch the Lord's anointed king." And he let him go. The Lord had given David the power, but instead of being controlled by that power David chose to be controlled by the Lord.

Centuries later, a Son of David would make a similar choice. Surrendering the power that was ever His to exercise, this Descendant of King David allowed Himself to be arrested by wicked men, paraded through a mockery of a trial, and impaled naked and alone on a cruel instrument of death.

> . . . Though he was in the form of God, [he] did not count equality with God a thing to be grasped, but emptied himself, taking the form of a servant, being born in the likeness of men. And being found in human form he humbled himself and became obedient unto death, even death on a cross (Philippians 2:6-8).

> "Father, if you are willing, take this cup from me; yet not my will, but yours be done" (Luke 22:42 NIV).

A person after God's own heart is one who refuses to take advantage even when it appears that the Lord has set up a situation for him to do precisely that. Perhaps the Lord has placed us in a position of authority where we could suddenly take action against another person who has harmed us. Maybe we're in business and promoted over someone else and we think, "Aha! The moment of opportunity has arrived. Thank the Lord—here's my chance." The temptation seems irresistible.

When I was in Nicaragua I met a young magazine editor who had received Christ at a Bible study six months before. After a press conference, we had a cup of coffee together and the young journalist revealed a serious struggle he was going through.

"For years," he explained, "two newspaper men have been telling lies about me, trying to destroy me. Just recently I was going through some files and came across some things that could really sink both of these men. In the old days, I wouldn't have hesitated to run a cover-story 'exposé' on these guys."

"And now?" I asked.

"Well . . . now I'm in an awful struggle. Everything in me wants to lash back at those liars—to stick them. But you know, I felt by the Holy Spirit that I shouldn't do it. And yet that goes against all my training. What do you think I should do? Denounce them? Expose them? Really do them in? Or do nothing? I could lose my job if it came out that I sat on this story."

I said, "Now listen. You've obeyed the voice of the Spirit up to now. You'd better do what the Lord tells you to do."

Although what this editor was going to do was righteous, the reason he was going to do it was unrighteous. He had enough sensitivity to the Holy Spirit to hold back when he might have easily rammed in the dagger to the hilt. "Just wait on the Lord," I told him. "God has been working these things out down through history. He takes care of it in a beautiful way."

Before the third week of the crusade was over, the editor came back.

"Remember that counsel you gave me about not taking revenge on those two fellows?" he said. "You told me that the Lord probably had something planned that was much better—better than I could imagine. Señor Palau, do you know what happened? This week I got a call from the President. I'm being sent out of the country as an assistant ambassador!"

It was so exciting! God had taken care of the situation and the young man was kept from doing something he might have later regretted. His conscience was clear before God. The Bible says in Romans 12:19:

> Beloved, *never avenge yourselves, but leave it to the wrath of God; for it is written, "Vengeance is mine, I will repay, says the Lord."*

It says *never* take your own revenge. You say, "Do you mean *never*? Not even a little bit to show them I'm not dumb—that I know what's going on?" No. It says *never*. God will take care of it.

Now David knew that Saul was finished. He knew that he was going to be the next king. Even Saul's son Jonathan told him, "You're going to be the king. I'm going to be second to you." David knew it all—all the prophecies, all the indications. He knew he was going to be Number One. And it appeared normal to human nature to say, "Get him now, and you'll be king today! Why wait any more?" He had a right to kill Saul. It was war. Saul was out to get him. But David said, "Oh no. I'm not going to move one step ahead of the Lord." He was sensitive. That position of power that had turned Saul's heart from God turned David's heart to greater reliance upon his Lord. David's influence and might would greatly eclipse that of his predecessor, but it was a tempered strength—tempered by gentleness and by sensitivity to God's Spirit.

Think about it a minute. What is your reaction when God places you in a position of power? You say, "What power? I'm no king. I don't carry a sword around." No, but we all find ourselves in a position of advantage from time to time; as an officeholder at church, as a supervisor at work, as a parent, or as a wife or husband who knows right where that partner is most vulnerable. The moment of advantage—how we respond in that instant of power reveals volumes about our character and our walk with God. David surrendered his opportunity, his power, and his advantage to God. He turned back from following after vengeance, and kept right on pursuing God's heart. Which way are you running?

A WILLINGNESS TO ADMIT SIN

If Saul had not been king, he could have blamed all his troubles on the government. Unfortunately, he *was* the government. So he blamed the people instead. Constantly. He would tell God, "It's because of these people that such-and-such happened. I was just trying to please the people." He even had the audacity to blame Samuel the prophet. Saul said, "Well, you didn't show up on time. What else could I do?" Saul never admitted his sins; he was always quick to justify himself.

Not so with David. When the prophet pointed the finger at David's sin, it was like a hot poker on his chest. He cried out to God. In his spirit, he could immediately discern when God was speaking to him through another person.

In 1 Samuel 25, the one who spoke was a woman named Abigail. This one brave woman stepped in front of a vengeance-bent 400-man army, with David leading the pack. Putting one's self in the path of an inflamed company of fierce swordsmen would be like leaping from a subway platform in front of a speeding train. In those days, men of war didn't have much time for pleading women, especially when they were in the way. But Abigail was no ordinary woman and David was no average soldier. And—Abigail had a message.

Her foolish husband, Nabal, had just delivered a stinging rebuke to the exiled son of Jesse, returning David's kindness with a cold, insulting refusal to help. David's response?

> *"Every man gird on his sword!" And every man of them girded on his sword; David also girded on his sword; and about four hundred men went up after David (1 Samuel 25:13).*

David was on fire and his eyes were filled with visions of liquidating one wooden-headed sheep-rancher named Nabal.

Abigail, Nabal's unfortunate wife, got wind of the plan and immediately mounted her donkey in hopes of intercepting David's hardened band of outcast soldiers. Seeing David striding forward in cold fury, Abigail jumped off her donkey and bowed at David's feet. She knew David could have hewed her in two with his sword or walked over the top of her. When he didn't, she took that as a good sign and spoke up: "Sir, I know my husband is a mule and all that. I realize he deserves to be killed. But when you become king, what will happen to your memory if you cut down this foolish man? What will people say about you? You will have a stain on your hands. I beg you not to touch him. God will judge my husband."

David cooled down fast. The murderous anger faded from his eyes and he regarded this remarkable woman with amazement and appreciation. Recognizing the voice of God in Abigail's plea, David replied:

> Blessed be the LORD, the God of Israel, who sent you this day to meet me! Blessed be your discretion, and blessed be you, who have kept me this day from bloodguilt and from avenging myself with my own hand! For as surely as the LORD the God of Israel lives, who has restrained me from hurting you, unless you had made haste and come to meet me, truly by morning there had not been left to Nabal so much as one male (1 Samuel 25:32-34).

Here was a woman David had never met before.

And when she pointed out to him the folly of his course, the most feared man in Israel replied, "Thank you for coming. Thank you for stopping me. You are right. It would have been awful."

God took care of the situation; a few days later her husband Nabal died. Later on, David sent for Abigail and she willingly became his wife.

In Psalm 51 David said, "A broken and contrite heart, O God, thou wilt not despise." David always had a broken heart over his sin. He didn't point the finger like Saul—he allowed the finger to point at him. Even when he was king, on top of the pile, again and again David would come down from his throne, get on his knees, and admit, "I have sinned against the Lord." And the Lord always forgave him. You never find David defending himself like Saul did. You never see him trying to justify his own guilt. As soon as a sin or weakness was pointed out, he'd say, "You're right. I am to blame. God forgive me." That's the big difference.

So many people want to defend themselves, refusing to admit their guilt. We see homosexuals deny their sin and seek to explain away the clear and ringing condemnations of Scripture. It's the same with adultery. More and more people arrogantly challenge the strong voice of God's Word and say, "What's wrong with divorcing my wife and marrying another woman? God wants me to be happy. God wants me to have peace." Far worse than the act itself is the arrogance which defies God to His face. But when a person who has sinned is truly broken before God, agreeing with God over his sin and willing to change his direction, he will find cleansing and healing. The Lord is the first one (and in many cases the only one) to forgive him.

Have you ever had a broken heart over your sins? Have you ever really wept before the Lord? Not necessarily real tears, but inward tears—for your own sinfulness, agreeing with God that you were wrong?

David was not perfect, but he longed to be perfect. He desired to be holy. He prayed:

> Search me, O God, and know my heart;
> Try me and know my anxious thoughts;
> And see if there be any hurtful way in me,
> And lead me in the everlasting way
> (Psalm 139:23-24 NASB).

David not only agreed with God about his sins, in his heart he also wanted to agree with God about holiness. In Psalm 139 he says, "Oh God, Your thoughts are so beautiful. I could just spend hours counting them. If I start adding them up, they are more than the sand. Oh Lord, I hate sin. I hate it in others. I hate it in myself. Teach me, search my motives and my thoughts. Lord, show me what doesn't belong. Show me what makes You sad as You examine my life."

David was a soldier, a general, a wild character— but he was also a man with a tender heart who wanted to be holy.

Do you want to be holy? Or do you say, "Oh, forget holiness. It's too old-fashioned"? Do you long to be holy? Of course, we all have impure thoughts, and they often attack us when we're least expecting them. We all have moments when our attitudes are ugly and we hate ourselves for it. But the big question is this: Do you *want* to be holy? Do you *want* to be pure? Do you long to be clean? Do you long to be transparent before God and before people?

Get alone with God. Pray, "Oh God, I want to love holiness. Teach me how to be holy. Train my spirit to be thirsty for it like David was thirsty for it." As Christians, we are indwelt by God's Holy Spirit. Can you imagine a better teacher?

A HAPPY AND WORSHIPFUL HEART

We could note many other qualities of David which made him a man after God's heart. For one, David had a happy spirit. This doesn't mean he was *never* sorrowful or angry. David had plenty of opportunities to grieve—more than most of us. But there was something magnetic about him. He was the kind of man who could take 400 bitter outcasts and rebels into his following and before the year was out, transform them into a loyal army.

You can sense it in many of his psalms. Whether he was out in the hills, hiding in a cave, in the midst of battle, or sitting on his throne, David would pour out his heart to God. When he did, there was always room for praise and always room for getting excited about the greatness of God and His grace.

Sometimes it helps if we read these psalms in a translation different from the one we're used to. Otherwise, they are so familiar that they just roll off our tongues and never penetrate our hearts. Reading them in a fresh translation can make David's diary leap off the page at us. I grew up with the Spanish Bible; this translation to me is like the King James Version to many other people. I've known the Spanish Bible since preschool days. I could almost beat David to it when I'm reading. But when I get into a modern English translation, it's so refreshing that it seems completely new.

What is it like to live with *you*, to work next to *you* day after day? If you were to suddenly be taken to heaven, how would those who had been near you characterize your life? As a man with a happy and worshipful heart? As a woman who was a joy to be around? David was excited about life—excited about being a servant of God. And you know what? The Lord loves that. The Lord loves people. He is searching for those who will worship Him in spirit and in truth.

4

The Shepherd King

Before we considered the shepherd king, we had to look at the King's shepherd. Before we examined David over men it was necessary to see David under God. Now, having seen the man after God's own heart, we're ready to regard the king of God's own choice.

"You Did Not Choose Me . . ."

Remember what God said to Samuel after Saul had ruined his reign over Israel?

> How long will you grieve over Saul, since I have rejected him from being king over Israel? Fill your horn with oil, and go; I will send you to Jesse the Bethlehemite, for I have selected a king for Myself among his sons (1 Samuel 16:1 NASB).

How did David become king? The Lord said, *I have selected him.* David didn't become king because he pushed himself into it. He became king because God selected him to become king. It wasn't because some big-name prophet laid hands on David or poured oil over him and said, "This is he!" No, the son of Jesse was God's choice for the job.

When the prophet put his hands on him it was just a confirmation of something that the Lord had already settled. It was public affirmation before David's whole family, because otherwise they'd never have believed him. But as far as God was concerned, He had selected David while the teen-ager was still out in the hills with his father's sheep.

What a beautiful phrase: "I have selected a king for Myself." Don't leave those words in Hebrew history; don't file them away in a folder marked "Interesting Phrases." Remember, He selected you, too.

In John 15, the Son of David said:

> You did not choose me, but I chose you and appointed you that you should go and bear fruit (v. 16).

As those who belong to Jesus Christ, each of us can point back to a moment of decision in our lives, whether or not we remember the exact date and details. Maybe it was at a crusade or a camp or a church meeting, or maybe just alone in your kitchen. Wherever it was, at that moment, you gave your life to the Lord. That was your moment of decision, but the fact is, you were selected by God. What a comforting thought! I can never get over it. As I write these words, I am here because God selected me. And He's selected you. Don't wear yourself out trying to understand that concept. Just let it open a refreshing spring of encouragement in your spirit—right now.

The Lord says, "I want you to be one of My own. I

want you to be a king." Revelation 1:6 tells us that we are "kings and priests unto God." In other words, we can be kingly in our ways. Remember that! As a child of God you have dignity and infinite worth. You're not a worm, not some lowly creature who has to walk about all hunched over looking beaten and humiliated. You were selected by the King of kings and given a task that has implications for all eternity, no matter who you are, no matter how unimportant and insignificant you are in your own estimation.

Then secondly, the Lord not only selected David to be king, but in 1 Samuel 16:3 He says:

> *Invite Jesse to the sacrifice, and I will show you what you shall do; and you shall anoint for me him whom I name to you.*

God not only selected David, He *anointed* him. Bible teachers frequently point out that the anointing of oil is a picture of the Holy Spirit's presence in the lives of Christians. Each one of us who belongs to Christ has been selected and anointed by God Himself. But this anointing, this fulness of the Holy Spirit, is not something to flaunt before others. Rather, it is something to offer up to the Lord with gratitude and praise. We should say, "Lord Jesus, when You anointed me with Your Spirit, You anointed me for Your honor, for Yourself. Glory to Your name!"

Remember these things when your Enemy, Satan, whispers in your ear that you are worthless and nothing in God's sight. It's a lie!

A LOVE FOR UNITING THE NATION

As the king of God's choice, David was gripped by the desire to bring unity to his fragmented country. Even today, Israel is one of the most divided nations on the face of the earth. Back then, each of the twelve tribes was always fighting the other. Even though the tribes were supposed to be one nation under God (to borrow a familiar phrase), they weren't. Judges would come and go. Judah would fight against this one and Reuben would fight against another. Only when an outside enemy attacked them would they unite to help one another.

Doesn't that sound like the denominational scene we see in churches today? You know, we resign ourselves to division until an outside enemy, like the communists, crashes in and threatens the whole church. Then it's, "Come on, let's huddle! Let's get our heads blown off together." As I've traveled around the world, it is interesting to note that in countries where the church is persecuted, people immediately forget about denominations. They never ask, "Are you Presbyterian, Baptist, Pentecostal, non-Pentecostal, anti-Pentecostal? . . ." No, they're just a little band of believers who help each other, hide each other, and cling together like brothers and sisters. And they are.

When David came to power in Israel, one of his great desires was to destroy the internal enemies and unite the nation. Remember, when the people of Israel came out of Egypt, God said, "Look, this is the territory I'm going to give to you. You move in step by step and take the land. You must completely push out all the people who are in the land that belongs to you."

But the people of Israel didn't do that. They (like Saul) kept the best of this and the best of that. They forgave this bunch and they forgave that bunch. Later on, all these forgiven bunches they'd been told to exterminate became their worst enemies. When David took over the throne, he was firmly committed to carry out the order God had issued to the Israelites hundreds of years before, to wipe the land clean of internal enemies. He wanted to rid Israel of idolatry and make the nation one.

And he did. By the grace of God, by the power of Jehovah, he took to war. He began to destroy the Philistines, the Amalekites, and all the rest that you read about. When his son Solomon came to the throne, the land was at peace and united. As Solomon ascended to power, his era would become a type—a picture—of the millennium. The son of David ruled over a peaceful, united kingdom.

David, a man after God's own heart, a king of God's own choice, had a deep inner desire for unity. He wanted Israel to become all that God had intended it to be and he knew that that could only happen when the nation was one. There is an important parallel here for Christians. You can never be fully a person after God's own heart if there are members of the Body of Christ that you can't tolerate. If they are born again, if they are redeemed by the death of Jesus on the cross, then they are part of the Body of Christ.

LOVE THE WHOLE BODY

There are many people who love like the Pharisees. They love those who love them. But they have no tolerance at all for anybody who is "different." Few people love *all* the Body of Christ. Those who do, rise quickly to the top into positions of church leadership. I've seen it happen again and again as I've traveled in sixty countries of the world. Very, very few people truly accept and love a brother in Christ simply because he is a brother in Christ. Usually they get to talking and start cutting up the pie over certain beliefs and practices—Calvinism or Arminianism, Pentecostal or non-Pentecostal, and on it goes.

Acts 20:28 says very clearly that the church—the Body of our Lord Jesus Christ—was purchased with Christ's own blood. Listen, if Jesus Christ bought me with His priceless blood and if someone doesn't like me, he is going to have a hard time facing Jesus Christ. Because Jesus gave His blood for me, that means I cost Him something. And He is going to love me even if I do make mistakes . . . and I do. He also redeemed you, even if you're obnoxious and hard to get along with. If you are redeemed, I will love you because you are redeemed.

Do you long to be God's person? If so, you ought to love the whole Body of Christ. This doesn't mean you'll agree on everything. Nor does it mean that you'll go around approving everything everybody else is doing. It isn't some phony, "love-for-all-mankind" sort of sentiment. It's not necessarily an emotional thing at all. It is rather allowing the Spirit of Christ to so control you that His love for His Body flows through you. Are you willing to allow Him to do this in your life?

I know many people who are just one step from breaking through to being great leaders, great servants of God, with great influence. Some of them are close friends of mine. But they will not budge on this one thing. They prefer to be anti-this or anti-that. And God will not—and cannot—pour out His full blessing on someone who doesn't genuinely love everyone redeemed by the blood of the cross. Think about this truth—let it grip you—before you settle back into the comfort and security of your little denominational corner. The issues at stake are greater than you imagine.

GOD AT THE CENTER

How often a simple, youthful walk with God becomes clouded and obscured by advancing age and success. If anyone could be rated a prime candidate for this sort of decline it would have to be David.

After all, it is one thing to walk with God when you're a lonely teen-age boy out in the wilderness with a flock of sheep. You would expect a certain amount of religious fervor from a sensitive young man who listened with awe to the rumbling thunderstorms and stayed awake in the night watching the stars. But what happens when the youthful exuberance begins to wear off? What happens when the young man is thrust into the public spotlight and weighed down with the responsibilities of family and government? What happens when the poor boy becomes a wealthy man and the lonely teenager becomes a national hero? What happens to zeal for God then?

Nothing, as far as David was concerned. The boy after God's own heart grew into the man after God's own heart. The zealous teen-ager became the zealous king. When David was a shepherd in the hill country he made it his practice to put Jehovah at the center of his thoughts, his songs, his joy, and his dreams. God was the center of his personal life. As king of all Israel, it was natural for the son of Jesse to make sure that God was at the very center of national life as well. One way he did this was by bringing the Ark of the Covenant to the national capital.

You will remember that the Ark of the Covenant was constructed for tabernacle worship while the children of Israel were still wandering with Moses in the wilderness. In their worship, it was a picture of God's presence. Indeed, God actually promised to speak to the children of Israel from the mercy seat between the wings of the cherubim which adorned the top of the Ark. The Ark was placed in a separate room of the tabernacle called the Holy of Holies which only the high priest could enter once a year. In this way, God met His people.

Carried into Canaan, the Ark was soon disregarded by the people of Israel. Later, during the time of the judges, they practically forgot the presence of God. The Ark was off somewhere. Nobody paid much attention to it except from time to time when some judge would come to shake things up a bit. Most of the time, however, the Ark was forgotten and the Lord was not in the center of national life.

When David became king, the nation of Israel was so bruised and battered by wars, troubles, and divisions that the presence of God was only a distant memory. With God out of the center, Israel lost its stability, unity, and national purpose. Drifting back and forth on the tides of human power and opinion, Israel's ship of state weathered constant bickering, animosity, and open hostility among the people.

And doesn't that happen among us, when an assembly of believers forgets its true focus? A church has some trouble and people gossip, talk, and debate. They stay up until midnight and have all-night "prayer" meetings. But actually their minds are already set in their own opinions—they are remembering the Lord very little.

Some relatives of mine had this sort of thing going on in their church. As I listened to them talk I thought to myself, "Thank you, Lord, for getting me out of that kind of circle." Their church was fighting over petty issues. They were obsessed with rule-keeping, ready to dismiss a young pastor who went to see a movie ("The Ten Commandments"). There wasn't any talk about the resurrection of the Lord Jesus, or of the great acts of God in our time, or about the power of the Holy Spirit, or of people coming to Christ.

Like a band of self-proclaimed vigilantes, these people went riding around the neighborhood on their white horses looking for specks in the eyes of their brethren. How foolish! Consumed with all the "negatives" their eyes wandered from the great

71

Positive in their very midst. Like the Israelites in the day of the judges, they lost their true focus and the great overriding purpose for their existence. And where was the Lord? Well, He certainly wasn't in the center.

I remember one congregational meeting I attended just before my wife and I went as missionaries to Colombia. It was really sad. One man got up and said, "The pastor has to go because of this and that." Then a woman got up and said, "That's right. Amen, brother." Weeping, the pastor's daughter got up and said, "My father is a good man. Why do you treat him this way?" On and on it went, into the night. Fighting, angry, bitter words. I thought, "Lord, is this the church of the living God? Listen to them!"

So often we forget that divisions arise because God doesn't have His rightful place in our midst. When the worship of God becomes secondary, bickering becomes primary. It happens every time. David saw this in Israel.

The young king's excitement was boundless as he brought the neglected and forgotten Ark back into a place of prominence in the City of David.

> *And David and all the house of Israel were making merry before the LORD with all their might, with songs and lyres and harps and tambourines and castanets and cymbals. . . . and David danced before the LORD with all his might; and David was girded with a linen ephod. So David and all the house of Israel brought up the ark of the LORD with shouting,*

and with the sound of the horn (2 Samuel 6:5,
14-15).

What a celebration! No one fell asleep in that service! Not a single husband thought about the football game he was missing on television. Not a single wife worried about the roast in the oven. And David? He forgot all about royal dignity and protocol. He didn't worry in the least about his public image. The ark of the living God was coming into town! And David danced "with all his might." With every ounce of strength and emotional intensity he possessed, David welcomed the return of God to His rightful place in Israel . . . at the center. Bringing back the ark was to be the first step of David's lifelong cherished dream: to build a temple for his God.

God is looking for people who dream those sorts of dreams, people who long for His glory. He wants to use people like David who put the Lord at the absolute center of their lives and goals. That's why God said of David, "Now there is a man after My own heart. He stumbles, he fails Me from time to time, but I can see the desire of his soul. He wants to put Me first—he wants to make Me the center."

Could you honestly say that about your life— your heart? It's one thing to stand up in a testimony meeting and say, "Ah yes, Jesus is Lord . . . Amen." But deep down—in your inner self—is it true that Jesus Christ is the center? Is He in the center of your plans? The center of your family? The center of your hopes and dreams? Does He fill your vision? Do you honestly have that inner confidence and rest that, no matter what you are going through, the Lord Jesus is dwelling in your heart by faith?

Listen to how Paul expressed it:

> *I have been crucified with Christ: and I myself no longer live, but Christ lives in me. And the real life I now have within this body is a result of my trusting in the Son of God, who loved me and gave himself for me (Galatians 2:20 TLB).*

David had that confidence that the Lord was at the center of his life. And the Lord poured out the blessing. Do you want the blessing of God on your life, your family? Take time for a spiritual inventory. What is it that dominates your dreams and fills your vision? Do you find your inner self cluttered with selfish ambitions and materialistic goals? Bring God back where He belongs. Place Him at the center. He has a way of putting a cluttered house in order.

SEEKING GOD'S MIND

A third quality of David's reign as king of Israel and king of God's choice is that he actively and persistently sought God's mind on military decisions. In 1 Samuel 23, David was confronted by hostile armies on two sides. On the one hand, he was preparing to rescue the town of Keilah from an invading force of Philistines. On the other hand, he was himself the object of an intense manhunt mounted by King Saul and David's fellow Israelites. On both occasions David sought the mind of God.

In other words, he didn't say, "All right, boys,

here's another crusade. Let's hit it. It's the will of God that we destroy these heretics. So let's go get them." No. He said, "Let's see what the Lord has to say."

> *Therefore David inquired of the LORD, "Shall I go and attack these Philistines?" And the LORD said to David, "Go and attack the Philistines and save Keilah" (1 Samuel 23:2).*

But David's men were restless when he broke the news to them. They weren't so sure they wanted to risk a commando raid on Keilah.

"We're running like rabbits from Israel's army and you talk about attacking Philistines? . . ."

That shook David up a little, so he went back to the Lord for confirmation. He said, "Lord, my friends say we shouldn't go. What do you say again? Okay, we'll go." It's beautiful to listen in on their conversation.

Even though David had fought many battles, defeating Goliath, the Philistines, and many other enemies, he didn't depend on old victories for new battles. David went back to the Lord for fresh instructions.

In my work as an evangelist, I must remind myself of how David constantly prayed over the battles he was facing. Often in our international crusades we find ourselves facing major decisions. In our excitement over a possible course of action, we're tempted sometimes to say, "Oh, we don't have to ask the Lord about this one. It's so obvious." Then when we fall flat on our faces and say, "What happened?"—it's obvious. Instead of consulting the

Lord we went ahead with the "obvious" which wasn't necessarily God's best for the moment.

If David had only applied this same principle to his domestic life—how different his family history might have been. David committed his military decisions to the Lord, but he neglected to consult God regarding marriage. He simply didn't pray about the women in his life. And that severely crippled his effectiveness for God.

This has happened to many people . . . not just David. People will pray about a job, a church, unsaved relatives, and the Sunday school lesson. But when it comes to choosing a girl friend (or a boy friend), they think, "That's my choice. God doesn't have to be involved." So they refuse, or carefully neglect, to speak to the Lord about this portion of their lives.

In Proverbs we read:

> *Above all that you guard, watch over your heart, for out of it are the sources of life (Proverbs 4:23 MLB).*

Often Christian parents neglect to commit this area of their children's lives to earnest prayer. They have their own ideas what they want for their son or daughter. If it's a daughter, they'll want her to marry a sharp doctor with a Porsche 914 and a new boat in the garage. Praying about it gets a little touchy. They say instead, "Let's just trust the Lord . . . but do it." So young people rush into marriage but in ten months or perhaps ten years they come back for counseling. Maybe they didn't marry that doctor but rather someone else they didn't pray about—and he or she turned out to be a drunk, an adulterer, or something else.

We need to learn from David's life—his triumphs—*and* his mistakes. That's why the Bible records all of it for us, so that we can profit from this man's heart for God and avoid the tragedies that nearly ruined him.

A Servant's Heart

From man's perspective, the tools one needs to carve out a position of leadership in the world include a good-looking face, lots of charisma, regular press bulletins, and a media-wise public relations man. But don't try to use those tools to get ahead in the kingdom of God. It won't work. The Holy Spirit won't allow it. What God looks for in the leader of His choice is a servant's heart. And if you have a servant's heart you can be greatly used of the Lord.

The servant heart of David was in evidence from his early teen-age years. While young David served his father in the fields with the sheep, the other sons of Jesse were trying army careers. Eliab, Abinadab, Shammah, and the rest of them would come home on a three-day liberty, strutting around town in their flashy uniforms, but David—well, you know—he was out with the sheep. Nevertheless, while Jesse's older sons were out on training maneuvers with King Saul, David was alone in the hills being trained by the God of Israel.

Isn't it great the way God ignores all of the rules (man's rules) to fulfill His perfect will? That's the exciting thing about following Christ. He's never worried about doing things in the expected way, going through all the ordinary channels. God finds His own channels. God writes His own methods. Sometimes we'd like to present God with our operating manual and tell Him, "Now, this is the way it's done. These are the rules. This is the kind of person for the job." But God chooses His own leaders! He doesn't care one whit if a man is a shepherd, or a fig picker, or a fisherman, or a tax collector. God is looking for a responsive heart. Ask Rahab the harlot. God isn't impressed in the least by job title, bank account, or standing in the community. God is searching for a servant's heart. And looking out across the hills of Israel, God's gaze went right past the eldest son Eliab with his flashy uniform to let His eyes rest on a teen-age shepherd. "Here's a man after my own heart," God said. "This lad is going to be king of all of them."

David could have said, "But Lord, taking care of sheep? Following them through the wilderness? How can I ever become king?" But it was right there in the pasture that the Lord was teaching him to be king. His hotshot brothers who were pushing their own careers, trying to step all over David, never got to be anything. When David came out to the battle-front they said, "What are you doing, showing off here? Get out of here, kid. Go back to your sheep." But after the Goliath incident, do you hear about the brothers any more? It's hard to even remember their names, isn't it?

When David's father asked him to carry some food to his brothers on the battlefield, he could have said, "Why should I take food to those guys?

They're always putting me down. I don't like them. Send one of the slaves." But David didn't say that. He said. "Yes, Father, I'll go." By obeying and carrying that picnic lunch to his brothers, what happened? He met Goliath. If he hadn't obeyed and done what Jesse asked him to do, he'd never have been on the battlefield at the right time, in the perfect timing of God. He would never have defeated Goliath and, humanly speaking, he would have spent the rest of his life taking care of sheep. But because he followed through, step by step, and he had a servant's heart in his tender years, everything fell into place. God saw to it.

You'll notice, too, that when David was asked to become an assistant to King Saul he had a humble servant's heart. David already knew he would be the next king. He'd already been anointed with oil by Samuel. And when they asked him to play the lyre, to soothe Saul's jangled nerves, he did it without a murmur. He didn't say, "Hey, listen, I'm the one who silenced that loud-mouthed Goliath. All the girls are singing songs about me. Why should I sit here playing the lyre for this nervous old king?" Instead, he said, "All right, if I've got to play for this king who's trying to kill me, I'll play."

FAITHFUL IN LITTLE

The Bible says that the person who is faithful in little things will also be faithful in much. Think about that. It was a "little thing" for David to faithfully tend his father's sheep, wasn't it? Yet, God was watching him. It was a "little thing" to carry a few loaves of bread to the battle line for his brothers. But God was preparing a marvelous opportunity for him.

What is a "little thing" and what is a "big thing"? Are there really little things, little responsibilities, little jobs in the service of Jesus Christ? Remember, our God doesn't measure as we measure. We look at publicity, national acclaim, and the public spotlight as the measure of success. God looks at faithfulness. What little things has God asked you to do? What little responsibilities have you been charged with? Do you feel neglected . . . shelved . . . forgotten? Give your task to God. Ask Him to help you attack it in His strength, with His perspective, reflecting His joy.

There are many great names in this world, attracting great attention and drawing great acclaim. God looks right past them in His search for little people in little jobs with great faithfulness and a great heart for Him. Are His eyes resting on you?

A Shepherd's Heart

Finally, we could note a fifth quality in David's reign as king of God's choice. The son of Jesse had a tender, shepherd's heart for his people. He may have been a rugged soldier who climbed all over the mountains of Judah like a wild goat. He may have been a politician who knew how to work the system and who could be cold and hard at times as the situation demanded. But in his heart, David loved the people of Israel. There was a tenderness there you may find surprising. He even called the people

. . . sheep.

This started back when he was a teen-ager and went against a gorilla named Goliath. He went out and said, "This Philistine is taunting the armies of God. He's a reproach to all of Israel. I'm going to tackle him in the name of the Lord."

He loved the people of Israel even when they were rotten, unruly, and ungrateful. Many of those people he risked his life fighting for didn't even want him as their king. In fact, for seven-and-a-half years after Saul died, only the tribe of Judah and Benjamin acknowledged him as king. Some of them said, "Who is David? Who is the son of Jesse?" Yet he continued to love the nation. When the rest of the tribes finally came around and acknowledged him as ruler, he didn't say, "Hey, where were you guys seven years ago? Now go fly a kite." Not David. Very humbly he said, "All right. I'll be king over you, too, if you want."

The depth of this man's love for the people is seen in his reign. For example, 1 Chronicles 21 relates the incident where Satan tempted David to take pride in the number of people in his kingdom. There is nothing inherently wrong with taking a census or keeping statistics. In fact, on another occasion God *commanded* David to count the people, even as He had commanded Moses to number the people at another point in Israel's history. What mattered here, however, was the *reason* David wanted to count the people. It was a matter of sinful pride.

It seems to me that it wasn't only David who got cocky about the big numbers, but also the people of Israel. They thought, "Look at that population figure. We are a big nation now. We can really defend our frontiers from the enemy. We can hold up our heads on the world scene. We've got the strength. We've got all these soldiers to fight the enemies. We've got David as general, Abner as his assistant. We can do it alone."

But God wasn't pleased. Even as the last figures from the last village were being tallied, God's anger fell upon David and the whole nation. He sent a pestilence which killed 70,000 people. They were dropping right and left.

> *And David lifted his eyes and saw the angel of the LORD standing between earth and heaven, and in his hand a drawn sword stretched out over Jerusalem. Then David and the elders, clothed in sackcloth, fell upon their faces.*

> *And David said to God, "Was it not I who gave command to number the people? It is I who have sinned and done very wickedly. But these sheep, what have they done? Let thy hand, I pray thee, O LORD my God, be against me and against my father's house; but let not the plague be upon thy people" (1 Chronicles 21:16-17).*

This is a touching incident. Remember, David wasn't afraid of blood. He'd killed plenty of people in battle and in raids on towns of enemies. But here he was faced with the knowledge that he had sinned against God. As a result, God was bringing a pestilence on the whole nation. David prayed, "Oh Lord, it's me. Chastise me. Punish me. Leave the sheep alone. I'm the only one who has it coming."

Notice that you don't find David praying, "Well, they had it coming, too. They're sinners. Let the Lord do it His way."

No, David really prayed his heart out for the people. He loved them like a shepherd. And God heard his prayer and stopped the pestilence.

It is interesting to compare David with his son Solomon who was, in human terms, the greatest king in Israel's history. With his matchless wisdom and administrative genius, Solomon had the nation running like a precision timepiece. Besides that, Solomon had wealth and power and worldwide fame that his father never dreamed of. Both men figure highly in the annals of the nation called Israel. But only one was a man after God's own heart. And it wasn't Solomon.

Why not open your Bible and make your own list of character qualities from the life of this man David? Answer the question yourself: What made David a man after God's own heart? But don't stop there. It wasn't just for the sake of history that God left the list for us to discover. Down through the ages He's been looking for other men and women to leave mediocrity behind and follow Him with a whole heart. He's still looking.

5

All the King's Horses
All the King's Men

Remember the fall of Saul? It didn't happen in one cataclysmic tumble—one damburst deluge. It wasn't as if one morning over his oatmeal Saul decided that he would reject God and rebel against His prophets. Sin didn't destroy Saul in a flash flood—it ate him away by erosion. It wasn't a sudden house fire, it was more like termites. Maintaining his kingly exterior, Saul went empty inside. One sin led to another sin, one lie to another lie, one jealousy to another, one disobedience to another. Finally, there wasn't much left for the Philistines to conquer.

But then, you say, the fall of David must have been different. With Saul it was like a slow rust but with David it must have been like an instant crash. Like a falling star. After all, wasn't he the man after God's own heart? He must have taken his eyes off the road a minute, then—boom—he was in the ditch.

It didn't happen that way. No one falls "suddenly." Not even David. Remember this: David's great sin did not happen in one impetuous, impulsive, momentous outburst of passion. David, like Saul, fell because of unjudged sin that finally caught up to blur his vision at a crucial moment.

Someone once told me, "Nobody becomes a leftist or a Marxist overnight. You go slowly from the right to the left, and one morning you wake up and realize you're a committed Marxist."

In the same way, nobody gets fat overnight. It's one pizza after another, one ice cream cone after another. And you hardly notice it until one of your children comes up, pokes you in the stomach, and says, "Dad, you've got a big belly."

Immorality begins with tiny things sown in your youth. Little things, little attitudes, little habits. Maybe some casual petting on a date, maybe some pornography that fell into your hands, maybe a fascination for sensual novels and stories. Little things. Yet if you don't crucify them—if you don't bring them to judgment—if you don't face up to them for what they are—SIN—they can destroy you. They can blur your moral judgment at a crucial, irreversible juncture in life.

When the massive Teton Dam in southeastern Idaho collapsed on June 5, 1976, everyone was stunned. Without warning, under clear skies, the huge earthen structure suddenly gave way, sending millions of gallons of water surging into the Snake River basin. A sudden catastrophe? An instantaneous disaster? It certainly seemed to be, from all outward appearances. But underneath, below the waterline where the engineers couldn't see, a hidden fault had been ever-so-gradually weakening the entire structure. It started small enough. Just a little weak spot, a little bit of erosion. No one saw it and it went untended. By the time the fault was detected, it was too late. The workmen on the dam barely had time to run for their lives and escape being swept away. No one saw the little flaw, but everyone saw the big collapse.

The record of David's moral collapse is recorded in 2 Samuel 11:1-12:15. It's all there, all the sordid details. We open our mouths in stunned silence as we read how "the man after God's own heart" raped another man's wife, tried to cover his dirty tracks, then turned around and murdered the woman's husband. We say, "How could it happen? David? 'The Sweet Psalmist of Israel'? I can't believe it."

We hear the same reaction in churches today when some glaring incident of sexual immorality within the assembly comes to the surface and takes everyone by surprise.

"Ahh—my! Such a fine-looking woman. No makeup, no wine-drinking, always took notes on the sermons, always listened to Bible cassettes in the car. And *she* ran off with *Harold*? Why, I was there when Harold was baptized. How could he do that? How could they do this?"

Some people say, "Well, they just stumbled." Come on, now. They didn't stumble. It was a planned move. The loud collapse that masks the hidden, neglected crack in the dam.

In soccer there's a little move some of the players use when the referee is looking the other way. They know how to deftly put a foot out to the side and trip another player who is running full-throttle downfield. It's very quick and neat and hard to spot when a player pulls it off. It looks just like the other guy stumbled over his own feet. When you talk about stumbling, people get the impression that this innocent young thing was just walking along when Satan put out a foot and—wham! She just fell over and . . . what can you say? You've heard the lines people come up with:

"Forgive me, dear husband. It wasn't a big thing. I'll never see the guy again."

"Elders of the church, it was just a little fall. You know how it is . . . I didn't mean it. Just receive me at the Lord's table again and it'll all be okay. I'm through with this other man . . . I just . . . stumbled."

Nonsense. Nobody falls into sex sin by chance. Nobody commits fornication, adultery, or homosexuality out of one sudden blast hitting him from somewhere. It builds up slowly, slowly, slowly. Falling is just the effect of the cumulative bundle of temptation and passion that has been piling up and has not been crucified. When the person falls, don't feel too sorry for him. You may weep, but don't feel sorry in that weak, sentimental sense that wants to cover things over. That person needs to bring his sin to the cross, to be broken before God, confessing it all. He must recognize that his sin is a loathsome thing in the sight of a holy God.

If we aren't hard on sin, then people will never break. They will try to pass it off. I've had people counsel me, "Tread easy, Luis. Tone it down a little. Some of these people have suffered enough—you'll hurt their feelings." Yet allowing sin to be shoved to one side isn't helping the person at all—it's hurting him—dreadfully. The sin of immorality is a killing, cancerous thing. You're not doing any good for the person at all until you've helped him to see that he must be genuinely broken before God. Once the sin has been dealt with by the Lord, then the healing will come. But not until.

I Surrender All . . . Except . . .

But how did it happen to David? How is it that God's handpicked king failed so tragically? It really started years before, when David was young. Reviewing this remarkable life we see that the son of Jesse was a man committed to the reality of prayer. David prayed over nearly everything. He prayed before battles and after battles. He prayed about his enemies and his friends. He prayed for direction and dedication, for health and for happiness, in his highs and in his lows, in caves and in castles. He poured out everything before God. Except—never once in the Bible do you find David praying about his love life. Not once. Although he ended up with eight wives and numerous concubines, we have no record that David took these prospective marriages before God, seeking His counsel. It was one area of his life he never yielded, and it almost crushed him.

As human beings, we are composed of three parts: body, soul, and spirit. The spirit puts us in touch with God. The soul is our personality, the sum of intellect, emotions, and will.

David had a beautiful *spirit*. As you read the book of Psalms you feel compelled to say, "My, what a guy this David was. I'd love to have been his brother. I'd love to have carried his sword for him.

I'd do anything for him."

The *soul* of David is one of the most attractive in all the Old Testament record. His *intellect* was first class—what an incredible, creative mind! His emotions—well, he might have been a little wild at times, but he vividly expressed emotions at both ends of the spectrum. So you might say he kept an overall balance. The *will*? What David set his heart and mind to do usually got done. Witness Goliath.

But his *body*. That was something else. When it came to the battle over bodily passions, David became extremely careless. And he paid for it very, very dearly. He won tremendous victories in the spirit. In his soul, he was irresistible—everyone either loved him or stood in awe of him. But in his body, he was so woefully undisciplined that it wrecked his life and shattered his dreams.

That's why each one of us needs to watch all those areas in our lives.

We need to care for the spirit: memorize scripture, attend worship services, spend time praising God, go to Bible studies, and maybe attend Bible school. Do it all.

We need to care for the soul: keep the intellect clear, go as high as we can, write, read, have the best brain in the world; keep the emotions in balance; put the will under control of the Holy Spirit.

But we need to keep our body under subjection, too. That's where David faltered. He continually gave in to his bodily passions. When he found himself facing the Bathsheba temptation, he caved in all at once—with no hesitation. There was no inner resolve to resist, there was no inner voice to object.

90

David's undisciplined body shouted louder than his soul or spirit. So David listened. So David fell.

WAITING FOR GOD'S CHOICE

How crucial to put this area of our lives under the control and guidance of God's Holy Spirit. There's nothing more traumatic and nothing more sad than to see a Christian's marriage collapse in a great flood of bitterness, grief, and regret. I get so desperate in urging young Christian fellows and girls not to be stupid about sex and marriage. If there was ever a time they needed to consult their wise and loving Lord over any area, then this is the time and this is the area. But so often they don't.

Young people need to be on their knees before God, asking Him if they should marry, when they should marry, and whom they should marry. They should pray earnestly for God to show them the things that will make a good marriage partner. It's not beautiful eyes that make a good wife, nor is it a good-looking, curvy body. It isn't eyelashes that go twiddle-twiddle (they'll fall out later on). Remember, no matter how much jogging you do or how much yogurt you eat, that body is still going to get wrinkled and worn out. Man looks on the outward appearance but the Lord looks on the heart. Not that a good-looking girl or guy can't have a good-looking heart, too, but how carefully we should tread. You cannot trample the clear teaching of scripture even in *one* area of your life without having it catch up with you sooner or later.

For instance, you all know that the Bible says not

to marry unbelievers:

> Don't be teamed with those who do not love the
> Lord, for what do the people of God have in com-
> mon with the people of sin? How can light live
> with darkness? And what harmony can there be
> between Christ and the devil? How can a Chris-
> tian be a partner with one who doesn't believe?
> (2 Corinthians 6:14-15 TLB).

At one conference I was talking with a teen-age
girl whose parents had attended Bible school. As
we talked I could see they had already begun to
compromise this very clear principle.

The girl said, "I want to be a missionary. I had
such fun with the missionaries I met last week. I
love missionaries. You're a great missionary. My
folks support you. I just want to be a missionary in
Latin America."

It seemed like she was headed in that direction.
She spoke Spanish, had a good vocabulary, and
loved Latin America. Our conversation ran down,
so I pulled my usual with teen-agers, "Have you got
a boyfriend?"

"Sure!" she said with a smile.

"Is he a Christian?"

"Ah, hmmm, no."

"Drop him tonight," I said.

"Oh, no, I can't do that."

"Well," I said, "go on living in sin if you want."

"I don't live in sin," she said. "I love the Lord and
want to be a missionary."

"Look," I said, "if you're dating a nonbeliever,
forget about being a missionary. You're just playing

games. It's a sin to go with a nonbeliever."

"What's so wrong about it?" she asked. "I'm not going to marry him."

"Then, why are you going with him?"

"Oh, I'm not. . . ."

"You're playing around."

"No, no, I'm not playing around. I'm serious."

"Well, if you're serious, you're going to get married."

"No, no, I'm not going to get married."

"Well, then, you're playing around."

"No, I'm not playing around, it's just. . . ."

I said, "Now come on. Are you going to marry this man, or are you just going with him for kicks?"

She pulled all the typical excuses. I wrote them down.

Girl: "I have no intention of marrying him."

Me: "Why neck, then?"

Girl: "All my Christian girlfriends are going with non-Christian guys."

Me: "Let them go through hell. But why do you want to go through hell?"

Girl: "Besides, my boyfriend is under conviction. I'm witnessing to him."

Me: "Look, the best witness you could make would be to call him up tonight or at the latest tomorrow and say, 'Look, I've been thinking about our relationship and I see that I am in rebellion against the Word of God. I like you very much. But we can't go out any more, and certainly not go steady, because the Bible says I'm not supposed to marry an unbeliever. I don't want to put you on that I'm serious about you and want to marry you. It's

93

against God's will. I'm in sin. I've asked the Lord to forgive me and I've got to break it up.' "

She said, "It would be a poor testimony to break up with him."

I said, "What's so poor about that testimony?"

She said, "Well, if I break with him just like that, he'd be so shocked that he'd turn against the Gospel."

I said, "Well, let him turn against the Gospel. But you've got to obey the Word of God. Besides, he won't turn."

And then she pulled the biggest excuse: "But my mother and I are praying for him." The mother had been telling my wife Pat this, too. I said, "Well, then your mother and you are both in sin."

"Praying for my boyfriend is a sin?" she asked.

"Yes," I said. "In the sense that you are praying it is. You can't ask God to bless something which He is against."

That mother—a Bible school graduate, supporter of missionaries—is slowly leading her daughter into disobedience and is going to bring trouble for the girl's marriage. The mother should say, "Honey, if you want to pray for what's-his-name, first you have to break up with him, then we'll pray that he will meet Christ."

A lot of evangelical Christians and their children are going through hell because they disobeyed God's command about not being yoked with unbelievers. In His grace, the Lord may save that unbelieving partner later on. But I tell you, it isn't worth the years in between. And it isn't God's best.

David destroyed his life at this point. Scripture

clearly shows us that this tragedy haunts even God's choice people—young people with a heart for God. No one is immune. David had it all put together in the second most important decision in his life. He had it right in relationship to God—that's number one. But in number two—the person he was going to marry—he was careless.

Even though many men in that day took a number of wives it wasn't what God wanted. David knew it. All he had to do was look over in Deuteronomy 17:17 to read it in black and white: "And he shall not multiply wives for himself, lest his heart turn away." Here God is telling the people that the king He will raise up shouldn't have a lot of wives because they will turn his heart from God. Since his teen-age days David had known very well that he was going to be king. He also knew the law. But he chose to ignore this one little point. He couldn't get over his weakness for women.

If this had been a general command, rather than one addressed specifically to kings, David might have said, "Well, Lord, that law is for rabble—for the common people. If we didn't have these laws, our society would be a mess. But you know, I've been anointed king. I'll have the money to take care of all kinds of wives." But David couldn't have missed it—the law specified *kings*. And he broke God's law. Outright.

THE GALATIANS 6 PRINCIPLE

What happened to David after that? He dried up. Read it in Psalm 32:3-4:

> *When I declared not my sin, my body wasted*
>   *away*
> *through my groaning all day long.*
> *For day and night thy hand was heavy upon me;*
> *my strength was dried up as by the heat of*
>   *summer.*

As long as he didn't confess his sins, he said, his bones dried up. There is nothing that will dry up even the most excitable, talkative Christian like sexual immorality. He may keep up a good front and mouth the right words, but his bones dry up. He's dead inside. That's because the Holy Spirit is grieved. And there will be no more joy until restitution and restoration have been done before the Lord, before the assembly, and before everybody that was offended.

David was restored when he confessed—when he said to the Lord in the presence of the prophet, "I have sinned against the Lord." When he said that, the prophet immediately replied, "The Lord has forgiven your sins." Notice, though, what the prophet added:

> *Nevertheless, because by this deed you have utterly scorned the LORD, the child that is born to you shall die (2 Samuel 12:14).*

That's the Galatians 6 principle. There would be consequences to David's sin. You say, "Doesn't the Lord forgive? Doesn't the Lord restore?"

The answer is, "Yes . . . nevertheless. . . ." That's the Galatians 6 principle.

You say, "But isn't the Lord understanding and

compassionate and kind? Doesn't the Bible say that God is love?"

Yes . . . nevertheless. . . ." That's the Galatians 6 principle.

> *Do not be deceived: God cannot be mocked. A man reaps what he sows. The one who sows to please his sinful nature, from that nature will reap destruction; the one who sows to please the Spirit, from the Spirit will reap eternal life (Galatians 6:7-8 NIV).*

Whatever a man sows, he will reap. If he plants to please his own flesh, he will harvest a crop of death and destruction. If he plants to please the Spirit of God, he will harvest eternal life.

The Galatians 6 principle says that you are responsible for what you have sown and for what you are sowing. Even though you confess your sins before God and find forgiveness, the forces have been set in motion. You will reap what you sow.

Even though the Lord had "put away" David's sin, the consequences would still come back to haunt him, like a bitter tide.

"Now therefore," the Lord told David, "the sword shall never depart from your own house, because you have despised me, and have taken the wife of Uriah the Hittite to be your wife. . . ."

David had sown in blood; he would reap bloodshed in his own family. David had sown in immorality; he would live to see a horrible harvest of immorality in his own home.

Do you remember that old poem from your nursery rhyme days?

97

Humpty Dumpty sat on a wall,
Humpty Dumpty had a great fall.
All the king's horses,
And all the king's men,
Couldn't put Humpty Dumpty
Back together again.

There are some similarities between King David and Humpty Dumpty. The mythical egg-man started out in great shape. So did David. But the storybook character didn't quite have what it takes to sit on walls. David didn't have what it takes in the area of self-control. That area almost demolished him, put a brake on his upward career, brought a curse on his family, and created a fracture in the people of God.

There is one big difference between David and Humpty Dumpty, however. David had a King who put him back together again. Nevertheless, the cracks in the shell were there until the end. David never got to be what he could have been. We have no idea today, nor did David ever find out, what he missed out on because of his great fall.

But David was still David. The apple of God's eye was still the apple of God's eye. Broken and humbled before the One he had once served with burning zeal, the son of Jesse was ready to start back on the road he'd followed so fervently from his youth. The way he'd wandered so far away from. The way to God's heart.

And this is the beauty and hope and joy of serving our God. There is a way back. The road is still open through Christ. God's heart still yearns for our fellowship. Praise God that He is the God of the second chance . . . and the third . . . and three hundred and thirty-third.

The psalmist says it:

> *If thou, O LORD, shouldst mark iniquities,*
>   *Lord, who could stand?*
> *But there is forgiveness with thee,*
>   *that thou mayest be feared (Psalm 130:3-4).*

The storms would descend on this man David — fire storms of betrayal, persecution, grief, and disappointment. But David was ready now. He could look God in the face once again. He could write new songs for God's glory. And though the melody was now bittersweet, the theme was ever the same.

> *I wait for the LORD, my soul waits,*
>   *and in his word I hope;*
> *my soul waits for the LORD*
>   *more than watchmen for the morning,*
>   *more than watchmen for the morning.*
> *O Israel, hope in the LORD! (Psalm 130:5-7a).*

6

"I Have Called You Friends"

The man after God's heart had a heart for men. The son of Jesse stands strong and tall in the inspired record as a true and loyal friend. It makes sense, doesn't it? Can a man call himself the friend of God if he refuses friendship to men? If the Creator longs after the rebellious creature formed in His own image, can the one who walks with God hold himself aloof? It should not be considered extraordinary that the man who evidenced such a profound commitment to his God was a man who formed deep commitments to men.

THE LONGING FOR FRIENDSHIP

Knowing my own heart, I am convinced that all men dream of deep friendship with either one man or a small group of men. Something inside man longs for a soul-brother—a brother he would be willing to die for. I believe God wove such a desire into the innermost fabric of our beings. I can't speak for women, but I'm confident I speak for many, many men. There is that secret dream that if the circumstances demanded it, in spite of human selfishness and sinfulness, the man would surrender his life for a buddy.

Of course, this does not at all take away from the friendship of a man and his wife. My best friend in all the world is my wife, Pat. I wouldn't trade her for any friend, man or woman. Augustine once observed that when God saw Adam was lonely, He didn't create ten friends, but one wife. Yet, in spite of the fact that your wife is the closest of all human companions, there is a restless something under a man's skin which cries out for the trust and friendship of another man or men. Someone with whom he can do exploits. Someone to help him fight the world. Stick it out, win or lose, thick or thin.

Maybe that's what makes the David and Jonathan story hit a man at gut level. Maybe that's what makes that portion of God's Word so attractive and compelling. Civilizations have grown and crumbled away, awesome armies have marched and armies have fallen, once-mighty kings, commanders, and self-proclaimed emperors lie forgotten in ancient mud . . . but the friendship of David and Jonathan—after four thousand years—goes on winning hearts and conquering men.

What a remarkable friendship. Not that Jonathan was David's only friend, but these men loved each other until death.

THE EXAMPLE OF FRIENDSHIP

We've already relived that historic day when the youngest son of the Bethlehemite rancher toppled

Goliath with a single stone and led the hordes of Israel to rout the menacing Philistines. But there were a number of subplots to the Goliath story. One of the most noteworthy friendships of all time began that very day.

> *When he (David) had finished speaking to Saul, the soul of Jonathan was knit to the soul of David, and Jonathan loved him as his own soul. And Saul took him that day, and would not let him return to his father's house . . . And Jonathan stripped himself of the robe that was upon him, and gave it to David, and his armor, and even his sword and his bow and his girdle (1 Samuel 18:1-2, 4).*

These were men who by all rights should have been bitter rivals. Both had a claim to the throne of Israel, Jonathan by birth and David by the anointing of Samuel. In those days you didn't try to undercut your political rivals by bugging their offices or tapping their telephones or launching a smear campaign against them. You simply tried to kill them. By all means—by any means. But not David and Jonathan. There wasn't an ounce of competition between them. After Jonathan saw David defeat the enemy's champion, Saul's son felt his soul knit to the son of Jesse. It was an immediate, inseparable bond. Jonathan loved David as himself.

Then the Israelite prince did something totally unexpected—even incredible. In front of his father the king, in front of the general of the armies, in front of all Israel, Jonathan removed his royal garments, unbuckled his sword and the trappings which identified him as heir to the throne, and put them all at the feet of the teen-age shepherd.

Do you realize the implications of such an act? Perhaps you're thinking, "Hmm. Nice gesture. He gave his buddy a new suit. So what?"

Try to picture yourself in the following situation. Imagine you're visiting London and have the opportunity to tour Buckingham Palace. As you are following the guided tour through all the gilded rooms you are pleasantly surprised to see the entire royal family in all their regalia standing in one of the large halls. "Hey!" you say. "I didn't know *this* came with the tour." Your guide pauses, allowing everyone to drink it all in. As you're fishing in your pack for your pocket camera, you notice Prince Charles step forward and whisper something to one of the stone-faced honor guards. Suddenly the soldier summons you to come and kneel before the royal family. Stunned beyond words you leave your open-mouthed tour group and wobble your way over to their highnesses. As you kneel, the Prince of Wales dramatically strides forward, studies you for a moment, then whisks off his regal robe and wraps it across your shoulders. Before you can catch your breath, he slips his royal signet ring on your finger, places his golden scepter in your right hand, and sets his ancient crown on your head.

Can you visualize it? Then perhaps you can begin to understand the shock-waves that went through the ranks of Israel following Jonathan's symbolic act.

"David, my friend," Jonathan was saying,

"here's my commitment to you. Not even the throne will come between us!"

Instead of competing with one another, it seems as if they were constantly trying to promote one another. This is what friendship is all about. When a man loves another man or a woman loves another woman in such a way that they promote each other instead of themselves—this is a mark of the genuine article . . . real friendship.

THE LOYALTY OF FRIENDSHIP

The friendship of David and Jonathan grew up in the sunshine of a victory celebration. It grew strong under the dark skies of royal jealousy and political intrigue as the smile of Saul's favor curled into the sneer of suspicion. It didn't take long.

> As they were coming home, when David returned from slaying the Philistine, the women came out of all the cities of Israel, singing and dancing, to meet King Saul, with timbrels, with songs of joy, and with instruments of music. And the women sang to one another as they made merry,
> "Saul has slain his thousands,
> and David his ten thousands."
> And Saul was very angry, and this saying displeased him; he said, "They have ascribed to David ten thousands, and to me they have ascribed thousands; and what more can he have but the kingdom?" And Saul eyed David from that day on (1 Samuel 18:6-9).

The word went out. David, the instant hero, was a marked man. He didn't need his face on a "wanted" poster in all the post offices. The word just got around: Saul wanted to retire David—permanently. And anyone in Israel who wanted to gain an immediate five-level raise in his civil service rating without taking the exam knew what he had to do. David may as well have embroidered a target on the back of his coat.

But then . . . enter Jonathan. Knowing all too well the murderous level of his father's envy, the king's son scooped all his available courage and stepped up to bat for his new friend.

And Jonathan spoke well of David to Saul his father, and said to him, "Let not the king sin against his servant David; because he has not sinned against you, and because his deeds have been of good service to you" (1 Samuel 19:4).

Finding his father in one of those rare listening moods, the crown prince rehearsed David's valorous deeds on the nation's behalf. "Remember how you felt that day when David shut Goliath's big mouth—remember that, Dad? Hey—and remember how we took off after those Philistines and how they scattered like quail before the bowman? Remember how the wine flowed and how we laughed and danced and sang? Remember? And now you're trying to spill the blood of your servant David? The man who sings like an angel and strums his harp to heal your jangled nerves? Think about it, Dad. It doesn't add up. It doesn't make sense."

So Saul remembered and repented. For awhile.

But jealous kings have short memories when it comes to recalling their rivals' redeeming features. After a brief respite, Saul was at it again. This time when Jonathan intervened, it nearly cost him his life.

> Then Saul's anger was kindled against Jonathan, and he said to him, "You son of a perverse, rebellious woman, do I not know that you have chosen the son of Jesse to your own shame, and to the shame of your mother's nakedness? For as long as the son of Jesse lives upon the earth, neither you nor your kingdom shall be established. Therefore send and fetch him to me, for he shall surely die" (1 Samuel 20:30-31).

When Jonathan argued the point further, Saul hurled his spear at him and would have killed his own son if Jonathan had not been quick to dodge. As far as his friend David was concerned, Jonathan did not count his own life precious. He was fully willing to defend the son of Jesse before anyone — even to the point of death.

These two men were totally committed to each other, vowing that whoever survived and came out on top would protect the other's descendants. Jonathan, however, didn't have much doubt as to who would be number one. Once when David was hiding in the forest the son of Saul sought his friend to encourage him and "strengthen his hand in the Lord."

> And he said to him, "Fear not; for the hand of Saul my father shall not find you; you shall be

king over Israel, and I shall be next to you; Saul
my father also knows this" (1 Samuel 23:17).

Jonathan was saying, "David, it's going to be good. You and me. You'll be king and I'll stand at your right hand—no matter what. Israel will blossom, David. Can't you just see it?"

Jonathan had a dream. In his spirit he could see the beginnings of David's glory—a mighty and eternal dynasty. And Jonathan would not let his own ego or personal aspirations stand in the way of that dream's fulfillment. David would reign. Jonathan would be happy and content to surrender his own rights and stand at the side of God's chosen king. Willing to be number two. Willing to let God exalt as He would.

How beautiful it would be if there were more of this in the Body of Christ. Friendships unthreatened by overblown egos. Friendships unafraid of commitment. Friendships unshaken by pressure, hardship, or sudden turn of events. Friendships that speak the same words face to face or ten thousand miles apart.

When most of us speak of friendship or "fellowship," we're talking about something different than the bond that David and Jonathan enjoyed. We draw invisible lines within our friendships and say, "This far and no further. I will be your friend . . . as long as it doesn't cost me very much. I will be your friend . . . as long as it doesn't involve a heavy commitment. I will be your friend . . . until distance, promotion, or pressing activities draw us apart. I will be your friend . . . as long as it's convenient . . .

as long as it doesn't embarrass me or cramp my style . . . as long as it brings me personal pleasure. Beyond that, forget it."

We live in an age that says, "You only go around once in life, buddy, so grab all you can. Make a friend, marry a wife, raise a family until it looks like they're beginning to impede your progress, then—ditch them. Write them off. After all, you've got to watch out for old number one. So use anybody you must to get what you want. Then when they get in your way, kiss them goodbye."

That's the kind of world we live in. A world that's haughty and proud on the outside but crushed with loneliness and longing inside. God created within us the need for commitment and security in our relationships; in our relationship with God, in our relationship with family, and in our relationship with friends. To the point we remain true to our own commitments, to the point we are willing to sacrifice our own best interests to promote and build in other lives—to that point—we find our deepest longings fulfilled.

Jonathan and David vowed to care for one another's families, if something should happen to one of them. Jonathan could say, "Hey, Dave, if you go before I do, don't worry about your family. I'll take care of them like they were my own. So put it out of your mind, buddy. You can count on it." And David could say the same.

How about you? What if your "best friend" died today? What would you do? Send his wife a 75¢ sympathy card? Send a bunch of flowers that'll wilt in three days? Stop in for five minutes every six months to give your regards? What does friendship really mean to you? I fear that many of us really shine when it comes to loving in "word or speech," but slip out the back door when it comes to living "in deed and in truth."

How smoothly and glibly the words roll off our tongues. "I love you, brother. I love you, sister." "I'll be praying for you." "I enjoy your fellowship." Really? Examine your words of "love and commitment" very carefully. God does. One day we will stand before the throne of our Lord Jesus Christ to "render account for every careless word" we have spoken (Matthew 12:36).

What kind of friend are you?

THE TEAMWORK OF FRIENDSHIP

During the course of my world-wide evangelistic ministry the Lord has privileged me to work with a team of men. We're a bunch of sinners, saved by the grace of God, but we still live for each other and pray daily for each other.

Some of the men of the Team live 10,000 miles away in Argentina. Some are in Mexico, some in Guatemala, some in Ecuador, still others in Chile. Yet when we come together we hug each other— like a typical bunch of Latins—and enjoy working together as if it had only been a few weeks' separation.

It's a great thing when a group of people can work together like that. I have friends that I don't see for months but the moment we're together it's like we just had coffee last Tuesday. There's an immediate sense of closeness. David and Jonathan had such a friendship. And you know, if we were more like Jesus Christ, controlled by His indwelling presence, we would be more and more like that to more and more people. Not exclusively with one or two or three, but able to embrace more people.

Although you can't be close to everybody, because time doesn't allow it, your attitude can be warm and loving and kind. How I long to be that kind of person. The Lord Jesus can make us that kind of person because He lives within us as believers and He was and is the perfect Friend. Proverbs 18:24 states: "There are friends who pretend to be friends, but there is a friend who sticks closer than a brother." Down through the ages, the true followers of Jesus have found those words eminently true of their Master. Do you know Him as your Friend?

A few years ago, *Decision Magazine* featured a story about two single missionary men in Africa during the time of the Simba rebellion. At that particular time, admitting American citizenship was tantamount to signing your own death warrant. One of these two missionaries was a Britisher, who could have easily saved himself from an attacking mob by flashing his British passport. But, instead, he chose to stick by the American missionary man who was threatened with death. The Britisher hid his passport and successfully passed as American. When the Simbas came to bludgeon the American to death, the British man threw himself on his friend and was killed.

Friendship. It's more than sentiment. It's more

than exchanging Christmas cards and baby pictures. Jesus said, "Greater love has no man than this, that a man lay down his life for his friends" (John 15:13). Are you that kind of friend? It can only happen through Him.

THE GRIEF OF FRIENDSHIP

The common reaction to the dismay and destruction of our enemies is one of suppressed jubilation, if not open celebration. You recognize the need to look properly sober on the outside but it's hard to keep the corners of your mouth from a slight upward bend. Inside, you're thinking, "Oh boy, did he get his. Serves him right."

If anyone was entitled to a little smug satisfaction on the death of Saul, it would have to be David. Hunted and hounded by the jealous king for years on end, David would have had ample time to plan his victory celebration as he ran from one cave, cavern, or hole in the ground to another. Because of Saul, David was forced to flee for his life, endure separation from friends and family, survive in a hostile wilderness, and make a pact with his sworn enemies. How many nights had he shivered in the open air, driven from shelter, wondering which breath would be his last because of Saul's relentless, pursuing army? How many tears of loneliness, exhaustion, and despair had he shed alone in the wilds or in a damp cave in fear of Saul's sword? So when the news of Saul's destruction dropped in David's lap, was it any wonder that he . . . broke down and wept? Amazing! The least one might have expected would be a mixed reaction, for both Saul *and Jonathan* had met violent death at the hands of the Philistines. But David didn't pick and choose. He wept for both men.

> *Then David took hold of his clothes, and rent them; and so did all the men who were with him; and they mourned and wept and fasted until evening for Saul and for Jonathan his son and for the people of the LORD and for the house of Israel, because they had fallen by the sword (2 Samuel 1:11-12).*

Notice this. Remember who Saul was. Saul was David's enemy to the death, but Saul was the king. And the son of Jesse had an awe, respect, and loyalty for the anointed of God, whoever or whatever he may have been.

When David received the news in Ziklag, he could have easily replied with justified sarcasm, "Yeah, long live the king. I am the king!"

But David wept.

I wonder how many people who had so enthusiastically campaigned for Richard Nixon wept for him when he fell. We are such sometime friends. We'll stick with a man if he's a winner, but the moment he's in trouble we become candidates for an Olympic Gold Medal in backpedaling. We're all ready to support the next one who steps in the limelight. Let's face it, in our carnal human nature we're basically fickle and disloyal.

But not David. I'm convinced that loyalty of heart toward others is one of the things we must ask God to give us. Not only loyalty for your husband or wife—this is already in bad shape in our present society, where at the slightest provocation people opt for "no-fault" divorce—but loyalty for friends, for employers, for others in the Body of Christ.

Note carefully David's actions in the first few chapters of 2 Samuel. It would have been a natural response if David had placed the crown of Saul on his own head and proclaimed himself king of all Israel. Had he not been anointed of Samuel? But he didn't do that. After composing a tender memorial dirge for Saul and Jonathan, the son of Jesse got down on his knees.

> David inquired of the LORD, "Shall I go up into any of the cities of Judah?" And the LORD said to him, "Go up." David said, "To which shall I go up?" And he said, "To Hebron." So David went up there, and his two wives also (2 Samuel 2:1-2).

Instead of jumping on his own bandwagon and setting up campaign headquarters throughout Israel and Judah, David simply fell back on his Lord.

"Okay Lord, what now? Which way? I'm ready to roll or I'm ready to wait. It's up to you."

KINDNESS OF FRIENDSHIP

Even years later, David had not forgotten his devotion to Jonathan and Saul when he inquired, "Is there still any one left of the house of Saul, that I may show him kindness for Jonathan's sake?" (2 Samuel 9:1).

When told there was one, Jonathan's son

Mephibosheth who was crippled in both feet, David brought him into his own royal house and treated him as one of the king's sons. After all those years, David remembered the promise he had made to Jonathan, his friend. And this was something more than a passive observance of his vow, because David actually had to search for Mephibosheth, since the son of Jonathan had been in hiding.

To me, another very touching reflection of David's loyalty is that, although he brought Mephibosheth to the palace for Jonathan's sake, yet again and again he referred to the crippled man's grandfather, Saul. Years had elapsed, yet David remembered the time when, in the heat of the battle, he'd had Saul at his mercy. David had crept up behind Saul in a cave and snipped off a piece of his coat.

When they were back outside, David called to him, "Hey, Saul, look what I have." And Saul, in a moment of fake repentance, had said, "Oh, David my son, is that your voice? When you become king, swear to me that you will be merciful to my descendants."

In those days, when one king fell, the next king felt obliged to murder the rest of the family so that no one would rise up again. Yet David had promised Saul that he wouldn't do that. Once firmly established in his kingdom, David remembered the words of his vow to the dead man and told the crippled grandson of Saul, "For the sake of your grandfather and your father, you are going to eat at my table like a prince for the rest of your days." Mephibosheth was astounded. "I'm just a crippled dog. And you want me to sit at your table?"

In modern Red China the victims of political "purges" become "nonpersons." Not only are they executed and buried in unmarked graves, their names are methodically erased from all the history books in the land. Their faces disappear from old photographs. Old clippings are destroyed. It becomes as if they'd never existed at all. Mephibosheth must have felt like that.

"Hey, what are you doing, King David? Who am I? I'm a nothing—a nobody—a nonperson. Why should I look on the face of the king? Why should I eat bread with the king's sons?"

And David told him, "Mephibosheth, it's not because of anything great or small which you've done or which you've failed to do. I accept you because of your father. I accept you because I promised your grandfather. Enter now into the king's house and enjoy all the provisions on my table. You shall be as my son."

What a picture of what God the Father does for you and me. We enter into the Kingdom, because of Another. We could never earn the right at all. We sit at the King's table and eat the King's food on the merit of our relationship to Another. We are accepted in the Beloved. Crippled, broken, "nonpersons" in every sense of the word, He sought us out and called us to Himself. All we had to do was acknowledge His gracious invitation and accept His provision.

Mephibosheth could have rejected David's offer. He could have clung to his own poverty, misery, and obscurity, spitting on the king's messenger and spurning the king's message. And he would have been a fool. Have *you* accepted *your* King's astounding offer of pardon and provision? Have you taken time today to thank your Lord for seating a crippled soul like *you* at the table of the King?

> *How great is the love the Father has lavished on us, that we should be called children of God! (1 John 3:1 NIV).*

PERVERSION OF FRIENDSHIP

What the world cannot understand, it either dismisses or perverts. David's relationship with Jonathan was so pure, so unselfish, so deep, and so strong that people who have rejected God cannot believe it. "There must have been ulterior motives," they reason in their dark minds. "This relationship must have been homosexual."

You'll hear that twisted statement more often in these days of national decline. Because the mind apart from Jesus Christ cannot fathom the concept of a true, selfless, Christlike friendship, it bends and distorts the truth of Scripture to fit its own warped philosophies. Militant homosexuals even have the audacity to use the relationship of Jonathan and David as a "proof-text" for their godless, evil lifestyle.

I am astonished at how many Christians I've met in recent days who do not seem to have any Biblical convictions about pure friendship or about the corruption of homosexuality or lesbianism.

Even at Bible conferences, people have come up

to my wife and me and said, "There's nothing in the Bible about homosexuality." Well, they must have an abridged edition or need to go in for an eye exam. There's enough in the Bible on this subject to build an airtight case against this ancient and persistent perversion. It is very, very clear.

Let's look at what the Bible specifically says about homosexuality. Take the time to read this passage very carefully. Don't skim—it's too important.

> The wrath of God is being revealed from heaven against all the godlessness and wickedness of men who suppress the truth by their wickedness, since what may be known about God is plain to them, because God has made it plain to them. For since the creation of the world God's invisible qualities—his eternal power and divine nature—have been clearly seen, being understood from what has been made, so that men are without excuse.

> For although they knew God, they neither glorified him as God nor gave thanks to him, but their thinking became futile and their foolish hearts were darkened. Although they claimed to be wise, they became fools and exchanged the glory of the immortal God for images made to look like mortal man and birds and animals and reptiles.

> Therefore God gave them over in the sinful desires of their hearts to sexual impurity for the degrading of their bodies with one another. They exchanged the truth of God for a lie, and

worshiped and served created things rather than the Creator—who is forever praised. Amen.

Because of this, God gave them over to shameful lusts. Even their women exchanged natural relations for unnatural ones. In the same way the men also abandoned natural relations with women and were inflamed with lust for one another. Men committed indecent acts with other men, and received in themselves the due penalty for their perversion.

Furthermore, since they did not think it worthwhile to retain the knowledge of God, he gave them over to a depraved mind, to do what ought not to be done (Romans 1:18-28 NIV).

In this powerful portion of Scripture, we're told that the final test of a homosexual man or woman who refuses to repent is that God gives him or her over to a depraved mind. *The Living Bible* paraphrases this well:

When they gave God up and would not even acknowledge him, God gave them up to doing everything their evil minds could think of (Romans 1:28 TLB).

People who indulge in this sin are exchanging God's truth for a lie. It's a damnable trade—and they know it. They know exactly what they are doing. Nature itself teaches what is right, but they switch it around to their own destruction.

Homosexuals worship the creature rather than

the Creator. They worship themselves, actually. They love to look at their own bodies. Therefore, God says to them, "You are turning My truth into a lie. You are worshiping your own body instead of Me—so go ahead and go all the way. If you've stubbornly set your mind in that direction, I'm not going to stop you. I'll let you see how it will be to serve your own depraved mind rather than serving your God."

Remember, this isn't easy for God. He loves lost men and women. He opened heaven and sent His Son to suffer and die for our sins such as these. But if a man or woman deliberately spurns that offer, trampling it underfoot, God will not violate that person's free will. Each man or woman must choose whom he or she will serve.

One hears fantastic, incredible arguments today. To some, they're so very reasonable. This is evidence of a depraved mind—so hardened against God that it has ceased to be ashamed of its own corruption. At least in the old days people were hypocritical. How much better to be a hypocrite and hide in the closet than to be a shameless person who openly flaunts immorality in the name of "personal rights" or "religious freedom." At least a hypocrite, by his very hypocrisy, is saying, "Listen man, I'm a pervert, but I'm not going to talk about it."

But the person who throws restraint aside, stands forward and says, "Gay is fun, gay is right, God loves gays . . .", God releases such people to serve their own depravity. And what a horrible tyrant to serve. Throw that door wide open and every imaginable sorrow and perversion crawls out of the darkness to stake a claim on what's left of that mind.

"Do you not know," says the Apostle Paul, "that the wicked will not inherit the kingdom of God? Do not be deceived: Neither the sexually immoral nor idolaters nor adulterers nor male prostitutes nor homosexual offenders nor thieves nor the greedy nor drunkards nor slanderers nor swindlers will inherit the kingdom of God" (1 Corinthians 6:9-10 NIV).

We need to learn those scriptures—commit them to memory—be alert. Not for the purpose of arguing but simply to be ready to use the Word of God in the power of the Holy Spirit. Unless God begins to do a new work in the Western world, these perversions will sweep in like a flood to erode the underpinnings of our society. Are you equipped, are you ready for the approaching storm?

What a refreshing thing to meditate on the friendship and love of David and Jonathan. Even in the midst of an age such as ours, this sort of loyal, abiding love is possible through the One who said, "Never will I leave you; never will I forsake you" (Hebrews 13:5 NIV). Because Jesus Christ called us to be His friends, we can experience the privilege of demonstrating true friendship to an incredulous, sin-weary world.

7

David
Had a Dream

Sometimes all it takes is a little storm. No thundering, sky-splitting tempest or howling hurricane—just a few dark clouds, a stiff breeze. And all the walls come crashing down.

Some people fall into a thousand pieces because of little things—the small hurts and tragedies which life regularly throws in the path of humankind.

But David withstood huge, catastrophic storms and terrible upheavals in his lifetime. How did he do it? How can you and I learn to face the inevitable major crises of life? David, for all his emotional ups and downs, had God-given perspective. David learned to look at situations—even heartbreaks—from God's point of view. He became great in the eyes of God and men because he sought God's perspective on the course of his nation and on history. Combined with a caring heart, this perspective reached out into a worldwide vision for serving the people of God.

WORLDWIDE VISION

These twin elements—a historical perspective and a worldwide vision—will lend stability to any life. The person who develops and maintains these qualities is not likely to fall victim to pressing circumstances and little storms. Although these may occur in his life, they will not destroy him because he is able to perceive a larger picture than the little box of his own pain and perplexity. He sees his life in the balance of history. Many people may encounter a little problem in their church, but they don't throw up their hands and think the world is at its end if they have the Bible's historical perspective.

Bombs explode at the Tel Aviv Airport and Egyptian troops move into position along the Suez, but the person with perception isn't panicked into thinking he's missed the Second Coming. In reading his Bible he realizes that many of the things happening today have happened before.

The most important thing is learning how to view both worldwide and personal crises and, further, learning how to handle them. The Christian asks, "How did the old brethren handle these things? I want to face them the same way. I want to learn from their mistakes and their victories and their faith" (see Hebrews 13:7).

Even though he didn't have television, newspapers, Rand-McNally maps, jet airplanes, or *Time* magazine, David had a historical perspective.

> *Why are the nations in an uproar,*
> *And the peoples devising a vain thing?*
> *The kings of the earth take their stand,*
> *And the rulers take counsel together*
> *Against the LORD and against His Anointed:*

"Let us tear their fetters apart,
And cast away their cords from us!"

He who sits in the heavens laughs,
The Lord scoffs at them.
Then He will speak to them in His anger
And terrify them in His fury:
"But as for Me, I have installed My King
Upon Zion, My holy mountain."

"I will surely tell of the decree of the LORD:
He said to Me, 'Thou art My Son,
Today I have begotten Thee.
Ask of Me, and I will surely give the nations as
Thine inheritance,
And the very ends of the earth as Thy
possession.
Thou shalt break them with a rod of iron,
Thou shalt shatter them like earthenware' "
(Psalm 2:1-9 NASB).

Note especially those last verses. We all know that this refers in part to Jesus Christ as the Messiah. But the exciting thing is this: Even though David didn't have instant knowledge about events taking place around the world, as we do, he had a worldwide vision and historical perspective. He was able to step back and evaluate the nations according to their relationship with God.

David asks, "Why are the nations in such an uproar? Why do they engage in these international conferences against the Lord and His Anointed? What do they expect to accomplish?" The nations may plot their strategies, they may issue their ultimatums regarding Jesus Christ and His Gospel, but God will simply laugh at them. He will scoff at them. He will look down at them and say, "Those little finite beings down there . . . they think they're going to put Me down. They think they're going to destroy the King. They must be joking, but they're not. So because they are not, I'm going to step all over them—I'm going to demolish them like a clay jar smashed on a rock."

The nations are still in an uproar today. You read of revolutions and wars, the Communist world, the Arab world, and the Western world. You see the forces that seem to be gathering for a third world war. But the Christian who has long-range historical perspective and worldwide vision doesn't panic like the non-Christian. He knows what's behind it all. And he is aware that God knows.

Notice how David wraps up that psalm:

> Now therefore, O kings, show discernment;
> Take warning, O judges of the earth.
> Worship the LORD with reverence,
> And rejoice with trembling.
> Do homage to the Son, lest He become angry,
>   and you perish in the way,
> For His wrath may soon be kindled.
> How blessed are all who take refuge in Him!
>   (2:10-12 NASB).

Even though David had a realistic perspective on how God viewed the warring nations, he also had a passion for those who didn't know his Lord. He wanted them to worship God, too.

I was eighteen years old in Argentina when I

began to really give my life over to the Lord. I attended a very small local church—only about 120 to 130 could squeeze into the chapel. Sometimes in the summer they opened the windows and those who couldn't fit inside would stand outside under the windows to listen. It was a good place for a teenager to be because they encouraged the young men to preach and gave us ample opportunity to practice. The elders would gather around afterwards and give us tips on how to improve our sermoncraft, delivery, and so on. But through my mother and some friends who prayed with me, I started to look beyond our little church in Argentina.

Psalm 22 began to get in my blood.

> All the ends of the earth shall remember and
>   turn to the LORD;
> and all the families of the nations shall worship
>   before him.
> For dominion belongs to the LORD, and he rules
>   over the nations.
> Yea, to him shall all the proud of the earth bow
>   down;
> before him shall bow all who go down to the
>   dust, and he who cannot keep himself alive.
> Posterity shall serve him; men shall tell of the
>   Lord to the coming generation,
> and proclaim his deliverance to a people yet
>   unborn, that he has wrought it (Psalm 22:27-
>   31).

In this psalm, David speaks of "the ends of the earth." Remember, in those days they didn't have TV, supersonic transport, or satellite mapping. Yet

David had a worldwide vision. Why? Because he'd been in the presence of God. He'd been taught by the Lord. Even though he didn't have a fraction of the scriptures we have today, David had enough to receive instruction from God. He saw that all the families of the nations would worship before the Lord.

A GLOBAL PERSPECTIVE

Herein lies an important key to maturity: Those who are really serious about the Lord's service ask Him for global vision and a historical, Biblical perspective.

When I read the paper, I don't get hung up on the political details of everything, but I try to see the hand of God in the movements of nations. When there is a revolution in some country, I try not to think of it as, "Oh well, another egomaniac gone berserk. Shot the king. Who's in charge now?" Instead, I try to ask myself, "Now what's God trying to do in that country? How will this affect the missionary effort in that area?" And even though I may have never met a person from that country in my life, I know I can pray for that nation.

Anyone who really gets involved in understanding God's worldwide activity cannot be content to simply sit back and think of his own pleasure. He's going to get a passion and a vision for the lost. David did—and that was thousands of years ago!

When I was a teen-ager, my mother kept saying, "There are so many millions of people who haven't heard about Jesus Christ. You've got to get out there, Luis. Let's have Sunday school. Let's have children's meetings. Start new churches." So we began to serve the Lord teaching children and then young people. We'd have all-night prayer meetings and would often get up at 5 a.m. to study the Bible.

VISION COMING TO PASS

In my late teens and early twenties the Lord began to put tremendous visions in my heart—intense desires to see not only the area around my home evangelized, but the whole city. Then, thanks to a missionary, that vision grew still larger and I began to think of the entire country of Argentina. Then the continent of Latin America. As my friends and I would pray, we asked the Lord that we would see three nations in our continent become fifty-one percent truly re-born evangelical Christian.

When we started praying it seemed like such a wild dream. But today, in three or four countries of Latin America, that prayer may be nearly answered. And I have faith to believe that with my own eyes I am going to see Christian presidents come to power in Latin America. Is it any wonder our vision is spreading to the whole world?

Whenever I speak at conferences or camps and get together with teen-agers who love the Lord Jesus, I often wonder if they have the same kind of passion in their souls for people outside of Christ. Every one of us can have it if we'll spend time in the presence of the Lord. When I was eighteen, the Lord began to bring into my mind the idea of working to evangelize millions of people through radio, television, and literature. But until I was thirty-two—even though the Lord had opportunities for me here and there—nothing very big seemed to break.

Those years seemed to last forever. We worked, we expected, we prayed, we planned. I filled notebooks with notes, charts, ideas, and plans. Sometimes it seemed the answer would never come. Yet in my soul, I knew God was bringing it about. I didn't know how. My mother was a widow and we were extremely poor. For years, I had to support my five sisters, my brother, and mother. Yet I knew that someday, somehow—God would do it. For twelve years I dreamed, prayed, planned, prepared notes—and waited.

David had a dream, I believe, that he would see the day when the earth would be filled with the glory of God as the waters cover the sea.

EVEN BEFORE KINGS

When I was eighteen I used to pray secretly, "Lord Jesus, use me to evangelize. Use me not only with children"—that's what I was doing at the time and there's nothing better to begin with than children—"not only with young people and adults, but Lord, grant me the privilege to witness for You before presidents, kings, and governors." I didn't tell a soul about this prayer, because others would have thought I was bigheaded. But in my heart I longed and prayed for this privilege. I said, "Lord Jesus, even if they kill me, I will tell them about the Gospel."

In the last five or six years, God has granted me the fulfillment of some of the grandest of these dreams. I've had repeated opportunities to sit before presidents, talking to them about the Lord Jesus as openly as I'd talk to any child out at a Bible camp. Of course, I treat them with more protocol, but it's the same Gospel.

Once the Lord opened a door for me to talk with the President of a South American republic at a Presidential Breakfast. Before it began, he inquired, "Palau, what are you going to talk about so I can think about a response?"

"Mr. President," I said, "I'm going to talk about the crises of the spirit."

"Crises!" the President frowned. "Let *me* tell you about crises!"

There I was, an evangelist, sitting beside the President whom I'd only met a few minutes earlier. And yet there he was openly sharing deep crises in his personal life.

As he talked, I thought to myself, "I can't believe it, Lord. This isn't some college student opening up here—this is the President of the republic pouring out his story, asking for counsel!"

Earlier, our team had gone to a Central American country and asked for an interview with the President. We were granted a ten-minute time slot but the President kept us for forty-five! As the conversation went on and became more personal, the President asked all his aides to leave the room. Only the President, two team members, and I remained. The President spoke slowly, with great feeling.

"The only answer to the problems of this country," he said, "is the message you people proclaim. There is no other option that will save our nation."

"That's what we feel is our contribution to the nation, Mr. President," I said. "We want to bring as many people as possible to a born-again experience with Christ. Then they'll be better citizens, and the nation will be a better place."

"I know it," he said. "I'm with you."

Do you know what happened? Two years later we went back to the western states of that nation. We drove into the number two city of the country and all over the city found posters that read, "The government invites you to come hear Luis Palau." My driver almost went in the ditch!

These posters had been printed on the government presses and put up by municipal workers at night—without a penny's cost to us. About 5,000 posters—put up because of a President's order to his public relations people. Because a President wanted his people to hear about Jesus Christ.

One night, as we came out of one of the crusade meetings, I noticed what I thought was a suspicious-looking character watching me in the shadows from the stadium. I said to those with me, "Watch out for that man—the one who's heading straight for his car. He's obviously in a hurry. Keep an eye on him."

When we got to our hotel, there he was in the shadows again out on the sidewalk. I ran to the room, rousted the other team members, and they went down and grabbed him.

"What do you want?" they demanded.

"The President sent me here!" the man said. This man was an assistant to the President for tourism. "If Mr. Palau needs a car, let me know," he said. "We also want to put him up in a decent hotel instead of this cheap place. We've also opened the northern borders so people can come in without papers to hear Mr. Palau's message. And he can come and evangelize any time he wants."

God just opened up the door. We hadn't even dared ask Him for something like that. You say, "All of this for an Argentine evangelist? How did it happen?" I believe it began to happen in my eighteenth year when I really started praying that whole nations would hear the Good News. I asked the Lord to do it. And the Lord has and *will yet* do it. Again and again.

SHINE WHERE YOU ARE

Luke 16:10 (NIV) says, "Whoever can be trusted with very little can also be trusted with much." So first, you shine where you are—reach everyone you can in your own "Jerusalem." Put your whole heart into whatever job the Lord has put into your hands to do, no matter how mundane or trivial it may seem. But pray big prayers—dream great dreams before your Father.

It doesn't mean that you have to be perfect before the Lord will use you. Just ask my wife if I'm perfect . . . she'll tell you! That verse does mean, however, that if you are trustworthy according to the light you have, if you are obedient to what the Lord lays before you each day, He will open another door of opportunity, and another. And yet another. The only limitations to our service in the kingdom are the ones that we impose, either by faithlessness or by lack of holiness or disobedience. Otherwise, any one of us could be used by God with mighty power.

Many of you know a certain country of South America persecuted and killed Christians as late as 1958. This was still going on when my wife and I and our two small sons went there to live. At that time, that nation had almost no missionaries. They hadn't returned after the violence that killed a quarter of a million people, including 135 preachers of the Gospel. Eighty-five chapels were bombed in those dark days.

It was tough to go. We felt we were ready even to die. We knew we could be butchered and our boys might be kidnapped. But we felt peace about going, and in praying with our field director we believed that this particular violent nation was going to open up and the whole nation was going to hear the Gospel.

A Jesuit priest had documented how at that time the government and church had a plan to destroy all Protestant Christians. Their plan almost succeeded, except—as in Psalm 2—the Lord laughed.

The Lord moved in and, with the help of many of that nation's youth, we began to have street meetings and crusades. The young people organized a youth crusade and planned to have a parade right down the main street of the capital city. They carried signs that read, "I believe in Jesus," and "Believe on the Lord Jesus Christ." A local radio station played a record of Gospel songs during the parade and everyone carried a transistor radio so they could sing in unison as they paraded down the main street.

We didn't know if anybody would come or what the police would do. It was a dangerous move. Because I had challenged the young people to do it in the first place, they asked me to be the evangelist for the crusade and I had to walk up in front of the parade. I thought, "Boy, this is a great way to go!" There I was, with a transistor radio, singing "Onward Christian Soldiers" and wondering where the police were going to come from.

We started out with about 7,000, mostly youth, and a few adults. They had come from all over the nation. As we started marching, more and more people joined in. It was a holiday—the Day of the Virgin—so they joined in, many not knowing what our parade was all about. Even six priests joined the parade!

When we got to the main plaza in the heart of the city, about 20,000 people were there. Later one of my friends told me that I stood on the steps of the capitol building and just laughed. I can't remember doing anything like that, but I believe it! I was so excited that the day I had prayed for, for twelve years, had finally arrived. And the doors had opened in a massive way.

The President of the republic had an office right on that square. He came out to the edges of the crowd while we were singing "How Great Thou Art" and asked a Campus Crusade worker, "What in the world is this?"

"The evangelicals are just singing, Mr. President," he said. "They're going to put a wreath at the feet of the statue of Bolivar. And that fellow up there is going to make a speech."

"My goodness," the President said. "If these evangelicals can gather such a crowd in our capital city, they could get a President into office."

That really shook him. Today the country has some of the fastest-growing evangelical churches in the world. It all started through the faith and prayers of many Christians—we weren't the only ones—including the faithful missionaries who also were waiting for the Lord to open the doors for decades.

Other things have happened since then. Last year I stopped in that nation en route from a crusade in Peru to be at three nights of rallies and pastors' conferences. While we were there, we got a call from a former President who is also one of the wealthiest persons in the country. His family was among those which had backed the persecution of evangelical Christians only fifteen to twenty years before. I was invited to his office on the nineteenth floor of a high-rise building. We sat down, had some coffee and chit-chat, and finally got down to business. Our conversation stretched out for over three hours.

"We fear that the atheists are going to take our land," the man told me. "We have become convinced that the only message ideologically that can stop atheism and keep our families from falling apart is the Gospel that you evangelicals preach." This was coming from someone whose partisans had been behind the persecution against evangelicals not many years before!

As we talked, I explained to him that we'd just held in another country what we called a "Family Festival." At our "Family Festivals" we use television, radio, meetings, rallies, and counseling centers to help families.

"Palau," he said, "if you set up a nationwide Family Festival for our land, we'll foot much of the bill."

Now you might say, "That's a political move." I say, "If they're going to foot the bill, let them make their political moves. Meanwhile, we'll have a chance to preach the Gospel to twenty-five million people." The Lord can do anything. He can move granite mountains. The Lord can do it in our generation!

A few months following this encounter we were invited to be at a Presidential Banquet in that same capital city. The guest list read like a "Who's Who." Besides the President, those attending included three ex-Presidents, three presidential candidates, the top military officers, ambassadors from all over the world, and many wealthy people from across the country. I was asked to preach the Gospel for thirty minutes. The President said, "Palau, this message will be on national television." It was.

It's happening all over South America. People are coming to Christ, not by ones or twos as before, but by the dozens and hundreds and thousands.

BE PART OF A MIRACLE

You can have a part in a miracle like this. Maybe

you think, "Luis, I don't have all the gifts that you have. I'm not a public speaker. I don't get around like you do." That's not the point. You don't have to be a powerful speaker, or a visible, public person. Do you walk with God? Do you pray big prayers and dream big dreams? Any of us, as long as we begin to walk with God like David did, can be used of the Lord to shake up nations for the Gospel. You don't have to be a super-anything. The Lord does amazing things that you cannot understand.

David wanted to be used by God to bring his nation back to the Lord. And where did the Lord find him? Out in the pasture—a teen-ager herding a bunch of sheep. But David had a heart for God, a heart for people, a worldwide vision, and a long-range historical perspective. Even in those Old Testament days, David wanted to be used by God to bring people into a right relationship with Him.

Let me ask you: Do you feel that kind of passion for people to come to Christ? If you don't, what can you do about it? Pray about it. Get on your knees alone or with your spouse and say, "Lord, I want a passion for the lost. Sometimes I couldn't care less, Lord. And I know it's wrong not to care. Give me a love and a passion for people. Not only my neighbors and relatives, but the nations that I don't like at all. Give me a love for the lost."

In Psalm 51, David says, "Oh, Lord, cleanse me, forgive me, give me a willing spirit. Then I'll teach transgressors Your way and sinners will be converted to You." The Lord can use anybody who has that kind of heart. Even if you haven't had all the educational privileges that you wish you had—and that would be good to have—the Lord can use you. I don't have all the privileges of education that I wish I had and that I ought to have, but the Lord has seen fit to use me. I believe it's because I really want to be used. And He can do the same with you. The Lord can do mighty things through any one who is available—man or woman, young or old.

At Urbana '76 I told 17,000 Christian university students: "Get yourself a map, either of a nation that is on your heart, or even of the whole world, and begin to pray for nations. Begin to invest time and thought in whole nations. Intercession is spiritual work and by praying in the Holy Spirit you can bind the powers of darkness. Pray until the outline of a nation's map is burned as by fire on your soul" (see Romans 15:30-33).

Through prayer, you can actually stay the hand of Satan (see Daniel 9-10). I believe that you can even depose governments by prayer in the Holy Spirit. Few of us have ever learned or practiced that. Maybe God will never take you to India or Pakistan, but He can use you to open up those countries for Jesus Christ and His Gospel through prayer.

I remember when I first visited the United States. I went to a missions conference in Michigan and met a missionary from Pakistan. I got a burden to pray for Pakistan even though my mission and evangelistic work were all in Latin America. As I prayed, I figured that some day the Lord would take me to Pakistan and to India to preach the Gospel of Jesus Christ.

Sixteen years have passed since then, and now I have invitations to go on preaching campaigns to several big cities in India.

When we were in Essen, Germany, one of the greatest joys of the crusade was when I met a Pakistani fellow by the name of Abdul, studying in Germany to be an engineer. During the crusade, Abdul gave his life to the Lord Jesus. I have a picture of him—a very handsome Pakistani. I said to him, "You know, you are the first Pakistani I have ever led to Jesus. For me, this is a fulfillment of prayer. I believe God is going to take me to your country. I've been praying for Pakistan for sixteen years."

He looked at me and said, "Would you repeat that?"

"I've been praying for Pakistan for sixteen years," I said.

"Why would you pray for Pakistan for sixteen years?" He was moved.

"Just because I love you even though I didn't know any of you. I just got this burden from God."

This man began to cry. "Then I'll help you win Pakistan for Christ," he said. He'd been saved for only five minutes and already he had a vision for his country.

The Lord can do miraculous things with our lives. We have to allow Him room to work. Our problem is this: Instead of presenting ourselves as those "alive from the dead" we waste time with our television sets and our trite jokes and our little holidays and we don't get the big picture. We mouth the words and say we're available to be used of God— but how could He get through to us if He actually wanted to use us?

Do you remember when David Wilkerson first

sensed God's call to minister to the hardened gang members in the back streets of New York? That came about after he decided to sell his television set and use the hours he normally watched TV as a special nightly prayer time before God. One night while he was on his knees in the former TV room, the Lord challenged him with this great ministry opportunity. What am I saying—that everyone should go out and sell their television sets? That's not the point. The question is: How open are you to the voice of God? How willing are you to pray and agonize over lost individuals outside of your own little circle of friends and family? How ready are you to start where you are and plunge into the work of touching lives for Christ in your own neighborhood in your own small way?

That's what King David had to do. He started as a teen-ager. When he got to be thirty, he took a segment of the kingdom. Finally, when he was thirty-seven, he took over the entire nation. The Lord gave him a name and success wherever he turned.

Do you have a worldwide vision? A long-range historical perspective? Do you see the nations with God's eyes when you read the newspaper, *Time*, *Newsweek*, and *U.S. News and World Report*? Do you look at unfolding world events and say, "What is my Father trying to do? What's He doing in Taiwan? What's He doing in Red China? And what about New York?"

You've got to get involved in the spiritual battle in the heavenly places. Read Ephesians 6:10-20. God can answer the prayers of some relatively unknown person and open up nations to Himself and for His glory. He did it through David. He's doing it today. He will do it through you. He wills to do so—do you?

8

A Sharp
and Ready Arrow

If David had the type of tombstone where they chisel an epitaph in the granite, what was said of him in Acts 13:36 would have served well:

> *For when David had served God's purpose in his own generation, he fell asleep; he was buried with his fathers and his body decayed (NIV).*

David served the purpose of God and he served his own generation. He died. He was buried.

And so it goes. People are born, live, die, and then their bodies decay. Many people brought up in the Western culture don't like to be around death. They can hardly wait for the mortuary to come and take away the body. These days, people usually die in hospitals, shut away from their families, and especially the children.

I was ten years old when my father died. They wanted to keep me away from the cemetery and burial ceremony, but I really wanted to go. So I jumped out the kitchen window and hid in the truck that went to the cemetery. Standing a little distance away, I watched them put the body of my father into the earth. It was a traumatic experience, but also one of the healthiest experiences of my life.

I knew my father died singing a hymn. He knew he was going to be with the Lord Jesus after he died. "Absent from the body, present with the Lord," the inerrant Word of God assures us (2 Corinthians 5:8). As I watched his body being put into the grave, I remembered how I'd been told that someday his body would be raised. Standing there alone in the cemetery, I believed it. It hurt a lot to know that I wouldn't see Dad for the rest of my life, but I knew he was better off than I was.

I'm glad I saw my dad buried. Even at that young age, it made me think very soberly about life. After that day, I knew that death was real, not just something that happens in the movies. I knew it happened to real people . . . to people you loved.

A REASON TO LIVE

Death happens all the time. It will happen to you unless the Lord returns first (1 Thessalonians 4). Maybe you're one of these persons who coasts along signing checks, shaving, bathing, eating, buying, selling, raising children, paying off the mortgage, and saying that's it—that's all there is. But is that really life? No. There's more than that. For those of us who are looking forward to being with Jesus Christ, life has a purpose.

David's life had a purpose; Acts 13:36 says so. His purpose was the purpose of God—*in his generation.* We can scream all we want about the mistakes of the past generation. We can dream and project ourselves all we want concerning the future generation. But there's nothing much we can do about either one. We can, however, have a dynamic effect on our own generation. We've only one generation to live in. Certainly, we may modify little bits of the past generations' actions. We will definitely influence some of the future ones. But God holds us accountable for *our* generation. In that is our purpose.

It's a beautiful thought. Every normal human being, anybody who has at least half his wits about him, actually wants to live a profitable, truthful, productive life. Only an absolute moron—a spiritual moron, especially—would want to just drift through life, pick up his paycheck, go on a holiday, get another paycheck, go on another holiday, and succumb to the illusion that this is all there is to life. Many people outside the Body of Christ live this way, but I can't imagine any true believer willing to just float down the river of life like an empty raft, ending up in the ocean or smashed to pieces on the rocks. It's so much better to serve God's purpose in our lives. And there is a purpose for each of us.

WEAPONS OF RIGHTEOUSNESS

There's a verse in Romans that doesn't even mention the name of David but speaks with authority as to the way he lived.

> *Do not offer the parts of your body to sin, as instruments of wickedness, but rather offer yourselves to God, as those who have been brought from death to life; and offer the parts of your*

*body to him as instruments of righteousness
(Romans 6:13 NIV).*

Another way to translate "instruments" is *weapons*. Then the verse would read: "Offer the parts of your body to him as weapons of righteousness." Isn't that powerful? That means I can actually pick myself up, so to speak, and present myself to God by saying, "Lord, I present my members to You, to be weapons of righteousness for You." To think that my eyes, my hands, my mouth, my mind, my emotions, my will—all can be weapons for God. What a motivating thought!

What about you? Are you a weapon of righteousness or unrighteousness? There is no middle ground. You can't say, "Oh well, on Sundays I am a weapon of righteousness, but the rest of the week I can coast a little bit, you know."

From his earliest years David wanted to be a powerful weapon in the hand of his God. And isn't it much better to decide to serve God from your youth? The holier you are from the earliest possible age, the more powerful a weapon in the hands of God you will be. God can use anybody. In fact, one time He decided to use a donkey. But God prefers to use holy, totally yielded people.

One of John Wesley's followers was Robert Murray M'Cheyne, a very powerful young man who died when he was only thirty years old. History has saved for us one of the letters he wrote to a man named Mr. Edwards. I have part of that letter written in the front of my Bible: "Mr. Edwards, according to your holiness, so shall be your success. A holy man is an awesome weapon in the hands of God."

An awesome weapon! Now, most of us would say we're anything but awesome. Nevertheless, we *can* be and Scripture says that we *are* weapons. How our Lord longs to hear us pray, "Dear God, here am I. Here are my members. Lord, I present them to You. Make them weapons of righteousness."

There's no telling what He will do with a life so yielded to His purposes. He can use you with mighty power, He may take you anywhere in the world, He may choose to do as He pleases, but you can count on one thing—He will turn you and your members into weapons of righteousness. Why don't you, right now, make a definite decision, based on Romans 12:1-2? Man or woman, whatever your age. The sooner you do it, the better. That way you'll avoid accumulating the scars, the bitter memories, and the haunting regrets of a life lived away from God. That's why I'm committed to youth crusades and meetings where the students and workers can dedicate their young, unscarred lives to God's purposes. They may not understand all that will come in the wake of that decision, but God will take them at their word, if they mean business, and He will really begin to use them.

NOT ABILITY, BUT AVAILABILITY

Perhaps you feel that you aren't clever, educated, or beautiful enough for the Lord to use you. My mind goes back to a situation at one of our crusades in Paraguay, South America, a few years ago. As

147

you may know, in each country when we have crusades we set up family counseling centers where people can come for spiritual help. One of our team members—the Rev. James M. Williams, M.A.—is in charge of setting up these centers and training local people to work in them. It is his usual practice to recruit pastors or professional people to work in the centers, people with a postgraduate education. Jim Williams looks for counselors who are trained not only in how to lead people to Christ but also in how to deal with deeper family problems, such as divorce, adultery, homosexuality, and so on.

At this particular crusade in Paraguay we had as many as seventy people at one time waiting at these family counseling centers for help. Since only about thirty-five had been trained to counsel, that meant not everybody could be helped at once.

As director, Jim got kind of nervous about that, especially since one of the people who took the counseling course was a "nonprofessional." This one man—we'll call him José—couldn't even read or write. But he loved the Lord and had a fantastic memory. He came to the counseling classes and when exam time came he knew all the answers because he had memorized them as the class went along! But because José couldn't read or write, like the other counselors, Jim asked the receptionist not to assign any cases to José unless they were really minor ones– because José might seriously misdirect the counselee.

One day all the counselors were busy and in came a very sharp-looking gentleman. He was obviously a white-collar individual, upper-middle-class. The only one left without a person to counsel was illiterate José. The secretary got flustered. José was alert, however, and walked right up and said, "I'll counsel with this gentleman." The secretary was too bashful and embarrassed to say, "No, José, let's call our supervisor, Mr. Williams."

So José sat down with this gentleman, talked with him, and led him to Jesus Christ. The fellow turned out to be a medical doctor. Meanwhile, the secretary had gotten through to Jim and explained the situation.

When the doctor and José came out after counseling, Jim over-eagerly greeted the doctor but just got a quick, perfunctory "Hello" in reply. Jim thought, "José must have really ruined that one." So Jim told the secretary, "Next time some distinguished-looking person like this comes in for counseling, make sure he goes to someone else. Don't give him to José. If I'm busy, come and call me anyway and I will take care of it."

The next day the same doctor returned, but this time he was accompanied by two men. These men were well-dressed and sharp-looking, apparently important people, too. The center was again extremely busy—except for this one illiterate brother who was sitting without anything to do. The secretary dashed off to get Jim and he hurried in and turned on the charm, "Oh, DOC-tor! How ARE you!"

The doctor said, "I want my two friends here to meet the gentleman who talked to me yesterday and helped me to receive Jesus Christ."

Jim said, "I'll be glad to take care of you."

"No," said the doctor, "I want José to talk to them."

So they had to get this illiterate brother and bring him in. Nobody knows what José said because the doctor wanted to be alone with him and his friends. But José led these other two men—who were also doctors—to faith in Jesus Christ. And the next day, to top it off, the three doctors got together and brought another friend who was having family problems. And this same illiterate brother led the fourth man to Christ.

The following week, the doctors had a party and the only one of the whole counseling staff they invited was humble, uneducated José.

Most of us would have responded as Jim did. We would have looked at José and thought, "This man is so incapable." He even needed his 12-year-old nephew to help him fill out decision cards. After he counseled, the little boy had to do the writing. But in three days the Lord used him to lead four doctors to Jesus. Who you are makes no difference to God, if you're available to Jesus Christ.

If a humble brother like José could be used of the Lord to win sophisticated, professional people to Christ—and they loved him so much they threw a party for him—listen, what could He do through you if you were surrendered to Him? What could He accomplish if you would say to Him, "Lord, I present You my body as a weapon for righteousness"?

That's what David did, and David served his own generation by the will of God. Then he fell asleep and he saw corruption. In other words, he died.

That was the end of David. Someday, that will be the end of us, too. When we die, the question will be: "Did you choose to serve the purpose of God in this generation, or did you choose to float along like a dead fish downstream?" The choice is yours.

Big Doors, Small Hinges

If you are a believer, the Lord surely has something for you to do. Something, perhaps, that will exceed your wildest imaginations. He'll do the abundant thing in your life, more than you could ever ask or think.

I was born and grew up in Argentina. I was a South American. I had no connections. I was the son of a widow and had to help support her financially. There was no chance, from a human standpoint, that my dreams of becoming an evangelist to masses of people across a continent would be fulfilled. But one day the Lord sent to our city two Americans I'd never heard of before. One was Dr. Dick Hillis and the other Dr. Ray Stedman. I was twenty-two then. Because I'd been to British boarding schools and knew English, I went to hear them. I went mostly out of curiosity, but something seemed to pull me in. After the meetings I went up to talk with these two Americans. Because of that simple encounter that lasted only thirty-six hours, the Lord opened vast doors to His glory. He soon moved me out of Argentina, and took me to Multnomah School of the Bible in Portland, Oregon. There I met my wife, Patricia. The doors opened, and more and more things began to happen.

I couldn't foresee any of that. I didn't twist God's arm or people's arms. I just waited for His timing. And you can do it, too. Psalm 37:3-5 belongs to all of us. That doesn't mean that some day you'll be preaching to presidents. The Lord may well have something better than that for you. There is an old saying I wish was in the Bible: "Big doors turn on small hinges."

When I went to that little meeting where Hillis and Stedman were speaking, I had absolutely no idea that my life would be thrust in a new, exciting direction beginning that very day. I simply went to that service because I felt an urge to do so, and now I see the Lord wanted me to. I might have stayed home and read a book or gone for a walk instead. How different my life would have been!

When Jesse sent the picnic lunch to his sons at the battle line, David might well have said, "Why should I risk my neck taking sandwiches to my brothers? Let them eat Army rations. I'm going back to my flocks." Then David might have never met Goliath . . . or his destiny.

Maybe you're waiting for the big break. And the big break never seems to come. There is an old saying that's been knocked around in the world for a long time: "It took me twenty years to become an overnight success." In other words, it doesn't happen overnight.

TRUST HIS TIMING

God simply wants you to be surrendered and available to Him, wherever He's placed you. Let

Him make you into a powerful weapon of right-eousness. If God decides to leave you in His quiver for a while instead of launching you at some great target—that's all right. Don't worry about it. He knows His business. You just concentrate on being His sharp and ready arrow—available for His timing and for His glory.

> *Wait for the LORD; be strong, and let your heart take courage; yea, wait for the LORD! (Psalm 27:14).*

Take that from someone who knows—David himself. Waiting for the Lord is the deepest proof of a heart after God.

Luis Palau is president of the Luis Palau Evangelistic Team, an international group of men whose worldwide ministry has as its stated objectives to preach Jesus Christ wherever the Lord leads; to stimulate, revive, and mobilize the church to effective evangelism; to plant new churches; and to inspire and encourage young men to go into full-time Christian work.

For further help and counsel, please write:

Dr. Luis Palau
P.O. Box 1173
Portland, OR 97207